ALSO BY STEPHANIE AND WILLIAM LASKA

The DIRTY, LAZY, KETO® Cookbook: Bend the Rules to Lose the Weight!
by Stephanie Laska, MEd, and William Laska (Simon & Schuster, 2020)

DIRTY, LAZY, KETO®: Get Started Losing Weight While Breaking the Rules
by Stephanie Laska (St. Martin's Essentials, 2020)

DIRTY, LAZY, KETO® Fast Food Guide: 10 Carbs or Less
by William Laska and Stephanie Laska, MEd (2018)

THE **DIRTY, LAZY, KETO®**

100 Easy Recipes to Save Money & Time!

DIRT CHEAP COOKBOOK

Stephanie Laska, MEd, and William Laska

ADAMS MEDIA

New York   London   Toronto   Sydney   New Delhi

Adams Media
An Imprint of Simon & Schuster, Inc.
57 Littlefield Street
Avon, Massachusetts 02322

First Adams Media trade paperback edition September 2020

ADAMS MEDIA and colophon are trademarks of Simon & Schuster.

For information about special discounts for bulk purchases, please contact Simon & Schuster Special Sales at 1-866-506-1949 or business@simonandschuster.com.

The Simon & Schuster Speakers Bureau can bring authors to your live event. For more information or to book an event contact the Simon & Schuster Speakers Bureau at 1-866-248-3049 or visit our website at www.simonspeakers.com.

Interior design by Colleen Cunningham
Interior photographs by James Stefiuk
Interior images © Getty Images/maglyvi, nadyaillyustrator, Serhii Sereda, Nadzeya_Dzivakova, petite_lili, LanaMay; 123RF/sudowoodo, macrovector, Aksana Chubis, Mikalai Manyshau
Author photos by William Laska

Manufactured in the United States of America

3 2020

Library of Congress Cataloging-in-Publication Data
Names: Laska, Stephanie, author. | Laska, William, author.
Title: The DIRTY, LAZY, KETO® dirt cheap cookbook / Stephanie Laska, MEd, and William Laska.
Description: First Adams Media trade paperback edition. | Avon, Massachusett: Adams Media, 2020.
Series: DIRTY, LAZY, KETO®. | Includes index.
Identifiers: LCCN 2020014550 | ISBN 9781507213896 (pb) | ISBN 9781507213902 (ebook)
Subjects: LCSH: Ketogenic diet--Recipes. | Low budget cooking--Recipes.
Classification: LCC RM237.73 .L373 2020 | DDC 641.5/6383--dc23
LC record available at https://lccn.loc.gov/2020014550

ISBN 978-1-5072-1389-6
ISBN 978-1-5072-1390-2 (ebook)

Always follow safety and commonsense cooking protocols while using kitchen utensils, operating ovens and stoves, and handling uncooked food. If children are assisting in the preparation of any recipe, they should always be supervised by an adult.

The information in this book should not be used for diagnosing or treating any health problem. Not all diet and exercise plans suit everyone. You should always consult a trained medical professional before starting a diet, taking any form of medication, or embarking on any fitness or weight training program. The author and publisher disclaim any liability arising directly or indirectly from the use of this book.

DEDICATION BY STEPHANIE LASKA

When I first started this journey, my goal was to tell as many people as possible about the benefits of DIRTY, LAZY, KETO. I created this lifestyle and lost 140 pounds, and I planned to spill all my weight loss secrets.

I was recently a guest on NBC's *Today* show. DIRTY, LAZY, KETO was invited to go mainstream, baby! In case you're curious about what goes on behind the scenes when appearing on a national television program, I'm going to give you the skinny. While getting ready to board my plane to NYC, I had an impulse to check NBC.com to investigate who else might be appearing on the show. My stomach dropped to the floor and I almost fainted when I saw two of my two favorite stars on the planet listed next to my name on the roster: Tom Hanks and Oprah. Yes, I said OPRAH!

I was nervous enough before, but I now felt downright sick. I was sweating profusely and felt dizzy. I considered running back to my car and driving home. My self-doubt went into overdrive, and I began to panic. *I CAN'T DO THIS* went through my mind about a thousand times as my family dragged me down the gangway onto the plane and strapped me down into my seat. We were going to New York!

The next morning, we met the producers at the *Today* show for a practice run-through. Apparently, since I'd be cooking three meals from *The DIRTY, LAZY, KETO® Cookbook* on live TV for the "Make-Ahead Monday" segment, the crew felt it best that I come in early to practice (THEY WERE CORRECT!). Because it was a Sunday, the *Today* show was not filming. The set was quiet, with only a skeleton crew present. Three long tables were set up with (what seemed like) hundreds of *empty* glass bowls, skillets, and sticky notes. *Time to pretend-cook practice!*

Twenty minutes later, we were on our way. I left with more confidence, knowing where I'd be standing, how the food would be set up, and the timeline for the next morning. There was just one thing I couldn't figure out… *What would I say to Oprah?*

I could barely sleep that night. When the hair and makeup team arrived at my hotel room at 4:50 a.m., I could barely see straight! Does it really take that long to get camera-ready? (Or maybe I just needed a lot of help!) Before long, it was time to leave.

The next hour went by lightning fast. We were constantly in motion. Because I was so nervous, I asked the nice producer to take me to the ladies' room. She escorted me down a long corridor when her walkie-talkie buzzed, calling her back to the control room.

"Just wait here," she insisted before running away.

I was standing there all alone when I heard it… *the voice.*

It was Oprah.

Clear as day, her voice coming from just around the corner—*Oprah.*

Hundreds of life lessons, inspirational episodes, and moments where I laughed (or cried) with Oprah *all washed over me at once.* Oprah taught me to trust my instincts and always believe in myself. At home, above my computer, hangs a sticky note where I scrawled my favorite quote from Oprah: "What would I do if I weren't afraid of making a mistake, feeling rejected, looking foolish, or being alone?"

Then the weirdest thing happened. All of a sudden, I felt calm. Surprisingly, I didn't need to say anything to Oprah after all.

I knew exactly why I was on the *Today* show. *I knew what I needed to do.*

I would tell the awful truth. No matter what.

I realized the reason DIRTY, LAZY, KETO connects with so many people is because it's honest. It doesn't require fancy or expensive ingredients, and it doesn't judge people for the foods they choose to eat. Canned chicken can become pizza crust, for cryin' out loud—*you can have your sugar-free cake and eat it too!* I would march back to that green room with confidence. Oprah had spoken to me (*well, from around the corner*) and I had listened.

It was time to step into my authentic self and tell my story.

You don't have to be perfect to be successful.

This one's for you, Oprah.

DEDICATION BY WILLIAM LASKA

I'd like to dedicate this cookbook to those DIRTY, LAZY, KETO peeps like me who want simple and economical recipes that still taste AMAZING. Join my family in the DLK kitchen, and let's do this together! Special thanks to my social media advisors and liveliest recipe testers, Charlotte and Alex. Thank you for your patience and understanding while Mom and Dad embark on this keto journey to spread the word of this unbelievable way of eating that has such profound potential to change and save lives! #KetoOn

CONTENTS

* To discover what these recipe icons mean, turn to page 16

5. SOUPS AND SALADS

6. SNACKS

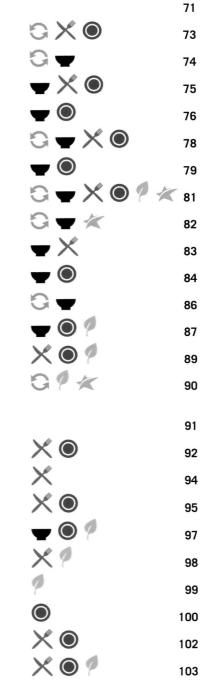

9. MAIN DISHES

10. DESSERTS AND DRINKS

PREFACE

Hear ye, hear ye! Are you a Strict Keto dropout? Do you live on a budget and feel like "healthy" food is out of your reach? Are you too intimidated to even start the stringent ketogenic eating plan? I empathize. The traditional ketogenic diet is complicated, requires upscale ingredients that cost a small fortune, and entails more math than you should ever have to do before you eat! *No, thank you!* But all is not lost. I've been where you are, searching desperately for an easier, more affordable way to lose weight. Gather round. Let me welcome you to a laid-back tribe called DIRTY, LAZY, KETO. We don't have matching jackets (yet), but you can easily recognize members of my group since we share a common belief system. (Plus, we walk with a skinny-jean swagger.)

> Our motto: "You don't have to be perfect (or rich) to be successful at weight loss!"

Call us weight loss rebels if you want to. This way of eating bends (and even *breaks*) the traditional rules about what we are *supposed* to eat. And do you want to know the biggest surprise of all? DIRTY, LAZY, KETO can be done on a shoestring. Put away your credit card as there is *absolutely nothing* fancy or expensive required.

Like many of you, over the years I've fallen prey to the hottest dieting gimmicks. Oh, the money I've wasted! Membership plans, prepackaged food, supplements, and hard-to-find specialty ingredients...*all under the guise of guaranteed weight loss in "three-E-Z payments."* Been there—done that! Oh, what a sucker I've been. Truth be told, I tried so many programs because I felt desperate;

I would've tried just about anything to lose weight. I gladly handed over my pocketbook (and pride). They made it sound so easy.

I had just about given up and then after a lot of trial and error, I created a new option. I wasn't following any fancy nutritional theories; in fact, I made up DLK on the fly. I experimented by eating a little of this and a lot of that, and made notes about what foods helped me to lose weight (while staying satisfied). And all the while I shopped at discount grocery stores. That's right: I didn't go crazy buying expensive "health" foods. I continued to buy regular "REAL people" food that my family would like (and I could afford!) on my limited budget. My discoveries surprised and delighted me. I would laugh out loud when standing on the scale.

"How is this *possible?*" I wondered. "Who eats mayo, sour cream, cheese, and nuts, but loses weight?"

I consistently lost around 10 pounds a month—for a year and a half straight.

I lost 140 pounds in all, half of my entire body weight. Amazing!

The gloves were off! When it came to my food choices, I played "dirty." No ingredient or food was off-limits as long as I could make it work in my daily net carb allowance. I could pop a Diet

Coke and enjoy a sandwich wrapped in a low-carb tortilla without shame or guilt. Heck, I could "hit a drive-thru" if I didn't feel like packing a lunch. *This made sense for my thrifty lifestyle.*

My new way of eating wasn't that complicated, either. Because of my self-diagnosed "point-tracker PTSD" from years following Weight Watchers, I refused to write down what I ate. Instead, I mentally kept an *honest* tally of how many net carbs I was eating. Admittedly, I laughed at my own casual behavior and often called myself lazy. Eventually, these two labels, "dirty" and "lazy" just kind of stuck!

DIRTY, LAZY, KETO enabled my 140-pound weight loss and continues to sustain my current, much healthier weight. With only a little fluctuation, I've been able to maintain the 140-pound loss for seven years now. For me, DIRTY, LAZY, KETO isn't just a weight loss plan; it's become a permanent way of life. And the best part is, I didn't go broke while doing it. There are ways to lose weight without buying expensive specialty foods, and I am living proof of that. My recipes use foods you most likely already have in your cupboard! Losing weight without added expense? What could be better than that?

Discoveries like this shouldn't be kept a secret. It would be an absolute travesty not to tell others who, like me, struggle with obesity. My mission is to shout as loudly as possible about DIRTY, LAZY, KETO. I promise to share everything I've learned, and not hold back. From the lifestyle lessons voiced in my free podcast, *DIRTY, LAZY, Girl*, to the detailed explanations and food lists shared in my "how-to" guide, *DIRTY, LAZY, KETO®: Get Started Losing Weight While Breaking the Rules*, I have already helped thousands of carb-addicted followers break free from the heavy carb shackles. There is an easier way that's affordable and doable for everyone; I'm going to help get you started *right now.*

INTRODUCTION

Losing weight doesn't have to be complicated or expensive.

When I created the DIRTY, LAZY, KETO way of eating, my family was surviving on a single income to pay the mortgage and car payment, and to outfit two demanding little kids. We didn't shop at fancy grocery stores, and there was usually a balance carried on our credit card. There was no room in the family budget to splurge on risky ingredients! Meals needed to be reliable crowd-pleasers or risk being fed to the dog under the table.

Rest assured, DIRTY, LAZY, KETO recipes draw upon the familiar. Every dish is created from the basics: *healthy fats, lean protein, and slow-burning carbs.* The ingredients are commonplace and likely already in your cupboard or refrigerator! There is no need to be suspicious; I don't joke about food! That's a subject too near and dear to my heart to pull those types of shenanigans. I do understand the reaction, however. When people hear I've lost 140 pounds with DIRTY, LAZY, KETO, they often assume I must be eating something uniquely potent. Magic shakes? Magic pills? Magic BEANS? *Nope.* Just regular food.

The recipes in this book are built around everyday ingredients that you can find in your local supermarket. Even better, they aren't expensive to make. I don't believe in pretentious meals. DIRTY, LAZY, KETO recipes are practical and easy to make. Don't confuse stress-free with skimping on taste. I love to eat, and my recipes taste delicious! Throughout *The DIRTY, LAZY, KETO® Dirt Cheap Cookbook*, you can expect to find oodles of helpful instructions and tips. I'm here to support you every step of the way.

I commit to provide you with:

- 100 easy-to-make recipes—there are no unnecessary steps or ingredients
- Recipes that are no more than 10 grams of net carbs per serving
- Recipes where you'll spend less than $10 per meal
- Helpful shortcuts for food prep and execution
- Macronutrients in line with DIRTY, LAZY, KETO beliefs
- Suggested tweaks and adjustments to add variety and suit personal tastes
- Entertainment, friendship, and support

Additionally, throughout the cookbook you'll find special awards that highlight unique attributes of the recipes, such as:

REBOOT: It's a *twofer*! Make extra and use part for another meal.

I'M HANGRY: Feeling *HANGRY*? High-fiber, large-portioned meals help "slow down" eating.

PICKY EATERS: *He likes it! She likes it!* Crowd-pleasing favorites.

FANCY ENOUGH FOR GUESTS: *Ooh la la…* Looks impressive and tastes great!

VEGETARIAN-"ISH": *"Kinda" meatless*, but may still call for dairy and/or eggs.

KETO SUPERSTARS: *Flick on your lighter!* Legendary rock star recipes take the stage.

The higher-fat, moderate-protein, lower-carb foods recommended by DIRTY, LAZY, KETO keep me full and satisfied. I have more energy than ever before! I wouldn't consider, even for a second, reverting back to my old habits. I've already wasted decades of my life suffering in denial about my addiction to high-carb foods. *No more!*

> For the first time in my entire life, I have a positive relationship with my body and how it is fueled.

And now you can too! It is an honor and a privilege to pass my knowledge on to you.

DIRTY, LAZY, KETO

SAVINGS

Lose Weight—Not Money

CHAPTER 1

THE DOWN AND DIRTY

EATING HEALTHY SHOULDN'T BE UNBEARABLE

When I was teaching elementary school, I would blast the song "That's Amore" when it was time to clean up from an art activity. I didn't have to say a word—the music would start, and the cleaning would begin. Can you picture a roomful of eight-year-olds putting away art supplies while swaying and singing along to Dean Martin? It was mesmerizing. Since I played the same song, at the exact time every day, the kids became programmed to tidy up when the mandolin struck its first chord. Those second graders are all grown up now, but I bet they still feel a Pavlovian response to pick up litter when this Italian jingle starts up.

As shown by my cleaning example, taking on a grievous task doesn't have to feel wretched. With a little reframing, even the most miserable activity can become joyful. This has been my approach to **DIRTY, LAZY, KETO.** If you can tolerate my artful jokes and outrageous recipe names, I'll try to make cooking healthy and losing weight enjoyable. Soon, like the hypnotized second graders, you will be singing the benefits of eating vegetables without any complaints.

> Having fun with cooking is easy, I think. It's the weight loss part that's really complicated.

Talking about weight loss can be an emotional minefield. If your childhood was anything like mine, you might have years of verbal abuse, bullying, and belittling under your belt from loved ones and strangers alike. Believe me, I understand how painful this topic can be. Like all good comics, though, I bury my pain in humor. Joking around has always been my coping mechanism.

LOSING WEIGHT SHOULDN'T BE COMPLICATED OR EXPENSIVE

Don't mistake my silliness, however, for incompetence. I love to eat so much and take food so seriously that I would never let you down! I stand behind every recipe inside *The DIRTY, LAZY, KETO® Dirt Cheap Cookbook*. I have only shared truly outstanding recipes here that I myself enjoy. Additionally, you will find that…

- My recipes call for everyday ingredients *you can actually pronounce*.
- You *won't* be driving all over town trying to find specialty foods—*who has time for that?*
- The directions are *simple* and easy to follow.
- Ingredients are so *common* they might already be in your kitchen.
- Every meal is *affordable*—nothing fancy or expensive here.

Because every recipe works out to be 10 grams of net carbs or less per serving, you won't have to worry about how the meal fits into your DIRTY, LAZY, KETO lifestyle. Put away your calculators because *the work has already been done for you!* **Macronutrients** (**fat, protein, carbs**, and **net carbs**) are clearly called out for each recipe and are 100 percent DLK-approved! Additionally, because this is a budget-themed cookbook, a breakdown of the "per serving cost" is also calculated.

DIRTY, LAZY, KETO IS DOABLE AND EFFECTIVE

Eating lower-carb foods that are higher in fat and moderate in protein can curb unnecessary snacking. It's not that these foods magically lead to weight loss—*that's not it at all.*

> DIRTY, LAZY, KETO meals leave you feeling satisfied. You won't feel deprived or resentful like you may have felt on past "diets."

How can you possibly feel angry when you're licking Alfredo sauce off your fork? *I mean, really.* High-fat foods taste delicious. No one can challenge that fact!

Another added benefit is how DIRTY, LAZY, KETO changes your hunger patterns.

> After finishing a meal, you feel full—and that "full" feeling lasts for *a very long time*!

If you've never struggled with your weight, that last part probably didn't make any sense to you, so let me explain. As a person who has wrestled with her weight for her entire life, I am going to give you a peek behind the curtain of what it's like to be addicted to carbs. I never felt full…*like, ever*! I could eat a bagel with cream cheese for breakfast, and then 15 minutes later be ready for another. It was like I didn't even eat the first breakfast; my level of hunger would be the same! My body might react differently to carbs than yours. That doesn't make me a bad person. I wasn't intentionally trying to sabotage my health by overeating. My body's reaction to carbs is likely due to insulin resistance, and that's definitely *not* my fault.

> Eating carbs *never* filled me up; they just made me feel *hungrier*.

Now you know, my friends, the secret of why DIRTY, LAZY, KETO is so effective. You will lose weight and keep it off because physically *and emotionally*, you aren't tempted to eat in excess. Doubt this way of eating all you want, but the physical proof stands before you. Sure, I've lost 140 pounds, but I have also helped thousands of others to do the same. *This works!* I explain the whole story in my first book, *DIRTY, LAZY, KETO®: Get Started Losing Weight While Breaking the Rules*.

LET'S BREAK IT DOWN—THE "DEETS"

Specifically, I recommend eating meals that are high in fat, moderate in protein, and low in carbs.

DIRTY, LAZY, KETO is NOT a "no-carb" diet—*that's Atkins.* Rather, I recommend enjoying carbs that are high in **fiber**—usually from healthy fruits and vegetables. Instead of overwhelming myself by counting **calories**, protein, fat, and carbs, I keep track of only net carbs. Net carbs are the carbs left over once grams of fiber and/or **sugar alcohols** are subtracted from total carbohydrates, per serving. I call this the **Lazy Keto** method of tracking.

When I was losing 140 pounds, I ate 20–50 grams of net carbs per day and consistently lost weight. Having a range (as opposed to a strict limit like with **Strict Keto**) gave me enough flexibility to live a normal life. This range proved tenable for the long haul. I'm still eating this way and it's been almost a decade.

THE DIRTY, LAZY, KETO FOOD PYRAMID

Before you head out to the store, take a minute and consider how this is all going to play out in the bigger picture. I don't want you wasting time or money picking out foods you don't need. Your time and money are precious! Let me help you make judicious and economical choices.

The DIRTY, LAZY, KETO Food Pyramid is not a defined step-by-step prescription; instead, it's a reference tool. Looking at a "day in the life" of DIRTY, LAZY, KETO, you will hopefully find inspiration for how to distribute your carbs across the food groups. By no means do you have to eat these exact foods! This is just a sample recommendation of how your net carbs might be enjoyed

AVOID

| Bread | Pasta | Sugar | Milk | Corn | Beans | Rice |

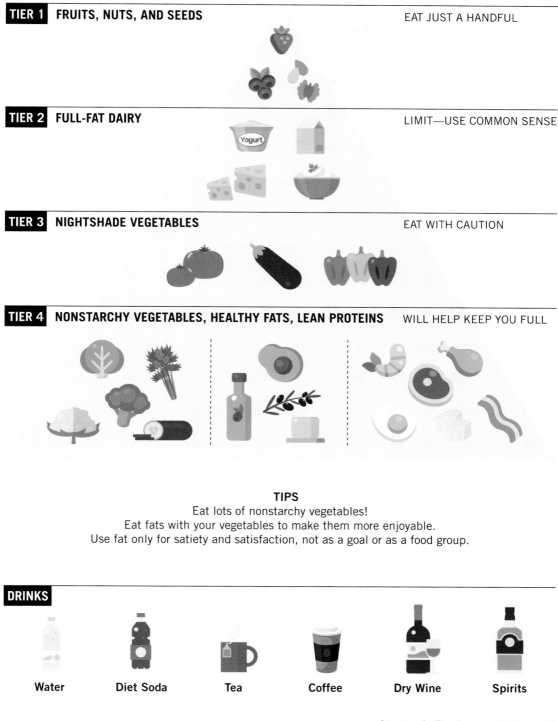

TIER 1 **FRUITS, NUTS, AND SEEDS** EAT JUST A HANDFUL

TIER 2 **FULL-FAT DAIRY** LIMIT—USE COMMON SENSE

TIER 3 **NIGHTSHADE VEGETABLES** EAT WITH CAUTION

TIER 4 **NONSTARCHY VEGETABLES, HEALTHY FATS, LEAN PROTEINS** WILL HELP KEEP YOU FULL

TIPS
Eat lots of nonstarchy vegetables!
Eat fats with your vegetables to make them more enjoyable.
Use fat only for satiety and satisfaction, not as a goal or as a food group.

DRINKS

Water   Diet Soda   Tea   Coffee   Dry Wine   Spirits

on a given day, given a sample range of 20–50 grams of net carbs per day.

For Some, DLK Is Controversial

Am I always in **ketosis**? *Probably not.* I don't think that matters. Critics always get fired up about this fact, to which I love to yell back, "WHO CARES?" As long as DIRTY, LAZY, KETO keeps my weight off, I'm fine with a little excitement. I don't have to be in ketosis 100 percent of the time. I'm betting that you will agree. It's impossible to be that perfect!

Before we move on, did you catch that bit about sugar alcohols? I want to make clear my position on sugar substitutes. I don't see anything wrong with using them.

> It's not a crime to drink a Diet Coke or chew sugar-free gum, so call off the **keto police**. *Let's get real!*

Dirty Keto empowers you to decide which ingredients or products to enjoy. Splenda, low-carb tortillas, and protein bars are all fair game. Hell, you might even enjoy a hot dog or a fast-food hamburger while still losing weight. *Your body, your choice!* Don't get me started.

I think you're ready! I promised we would be cooking here, so let's move on to the food. Most of us can identify how many calories are in the foods we eat, but with DIRTY, LAZY, KETO, there is so much more to consider.

NUTRITION LABELS ARE CONFUSING

Trying to accurately read a nutrition label can be confusing, overwhelming, and misleading. I'm just going to put that out there! You are not alone if you find yourself making mistakes. Even as the author of this book, I find myself reading and re-reading a label multiple times, often with exasperation. Sometimes, the data doesn't make sense. I've been known to yell at the package, "This *can't* be right!" or, worse, eat the food anyway (because I'm irritated).

Ironically, the regulated nutrition labels required by the government to *help* consumers make informed choices often lead to *confusion*, not clarity. Most of us lack training in food science and rely on the Nutrition Facts label for help. But the label has an overwhelming amount of facts and figures, wouldn't you agree? There are so many percentages! And long lists of ingredients we can't even pronounce.

As my son would say, "Mom, this looks like homework." (*Sigh…*)

If you're like me, you want to plow past the legalese to get to the bottom line.

> What we really want to know is: **Should I eat this, or not…** *right?*

Knowledge is power. I say, let's figure this out.

First up, how you read a label differs according to the country you are in. Unfortunately, there is no standardized, international label. Forgive me, international readers, but here I will use a US nutritional label for my example. You might have a laugh, though, as I'm going to point out my observations about the American nutrition information panel:

- Nutrition labels are mandatory for packaged foods, *but not alcoholic beverages* (so weird, right?).
- Most alcohol nutrition information found online is calculated with unrealistic measurements—*5 ounces of wine? Half a bottle of beer?* Not at my house, sir!
- The guidelines are in flux too, so just when you get the hang of it, they are updated.
- Serving sizes are almost comical—who splits a lunch-sized bag of Doritos into 2.5 servings? *Not on my watch!*
- Loopholes like "rounding" up or down mislead our expectations of what we are eating—*more on that in a bit.*
- Thankfully, one of the new regulatory changes Americans will see in 2020 is the callout of added sugars as a new line item. Now THAT actually sounds helpful!

With all that out of the way, you're ready to identify the key markers of a nutrition label with DIRTY, LAZY, KETO. Let's get started.

1   Notice the serving size.
2   Find the Total Carbohydrate number.
3   Subtract the amount of Dietary Fiber.
4   Subtract the amount of Sugar Alcohols (if applicable).
5   The result is the NET CARBS per serving.

Here's an example:

Nutrition Facts

Serving Size 1/2 Cup (64g)
Servings Per Container 4

Amount Per Serving

Calories 80	Calories from Fat 25

	% Daily Value*
Total Fat 2.5g	**4%**
Saturated Fat 1.5g	**8%**
Trans Fat 0g	
Cholesterol 45mg	**15%**
Sodium 110mg	**5%**
Total Carbohydrate 13g	**4%**
Dietary Fiber 2g	**8%**
Sugars 6g	
Sugar Alcohol 5g	
Protein 5g	**10%**
Vitamin A 2%	Vitamin C 0%
Calcium 10%	Iron 2%

*Percent Daily Values are based on a 2,000 calorie diet.

13
−2
−5
⑥

Paying attention to serving size is key. The exact amount of a serving is clearly spelled out on nutrition labels, but *not* in recipes. Why is that? There are too many variables involved with cooking to provide an exact amount. The size of eggs you use or the size of your pans directly affects how much food is made. But let's not overcomplicate this. In the spirit of Lazy Keto, put away your food scales and measuring cups when estimating what portion to serve yourself. Follow this simple calculation instead:

Divide the recipe quantity by the *yield* to determine the serving size.

If a lasagna serves eight people and has 9 grams of net carbs per serving, cut your lasagna into eight even pieces and enjoy. *Easy peasy!*

Are you wondering why DIRTY, LAZY, KETO subtracts fiber and sugar alcohols? Let's look into each of those in more detail.

FIBER IS YOUR FRIEND

Fiber is not digested by the body, so it's removed as waste. There are two types of fiber: soluble and insoluble. Besides weight loss, what are the benefits of fiber?

- Lowers cholesterol
- Decreases risk of heart disease
- Helps prevent spikes in blood sugar
- Supports a healthy gut
- Keeps bowel movements regular
- Gives you that "full" feeling

What's the difference between soluble fiber and insoluble fiber?

- **Soluble fiber** absorbs water. When you eat foods high in soluble fiber, it turns to mush inside your body. Soluble fiber absorbs water quickly and helps to soften stool while adding bulk.
- **Insoluble fiber** does NOT absorb water. Insoluble fiber moves through the intestine mostly intact, adding bulk to the stool.

The Dietary Guidelines for Americans recommend women eat 22–28 grams and men consume 28–33 grams of fiber every day, depending on your age. Personally, I eat even more than the daily recommendation for fiber. I find eating a balance of soluble and insoluble fiber safeguards against overeating, which is something I struggle with.

What are DIRTY, LAZY, KETO–friendly foods that are high in either soluble or insoluble fiber?

Almonds, raw (1 ounce)	0.7g soluble fiber	3.5g insoluble fiber
Artichoke, cooked (1 medium)	4.7g soluble fiber	1.8g insoluble fiber
Asparagus, cooked (½ cup)	1.7g soluble fiber	1.1g insoluble fiber
Blackberries (½ cup)	3.1g soluble fiber	0.07g insoluble fiber
Blueberries (1 cup)	1.7g soluble fiber	2.5g insoluble fiber
Broccoli, raw (½ cup)	1.3g soluble fiber	1.4g insoluble fiber
Brussels sprouts, cooked (1 cup)	1.7g soluble fiber	1.9g insoluble fiber
Flaxseeds (2 tablespoons)	2.7g soluble fiber	2.1g insoluble fiber
Kale, cooked (1 cup)	2.1g soluble fiber	5.1g insoluble fiber
Peanuts, dry roasted (1 ounce)	1.1g soluble fiber	1.2g insoluble fiber
Psyllium seed husks (2 tablespoons)	7.1g soluble fiber	0.9g insoluble fiber
Raspberries (½ cup)	0.9g soluble fiber	2.3g insoluble fiber
Sesame seeds (¼ cup)	0.7g soluble fiber	2.6g insoluble fiber
Soybeans, edamame (½ cup)	2.7g soluble fiber	2.2g insoluble fiber
Strawberries (1 cup)	1.8g soluble fiber	2.6g insoluble fiber
Sunflower seeds (¼ cup)	1.1g soluble fiber	1.9g insoluble fiber
Walnuts (1 ounce)	0.6g soluble fiber	2.5g insoluble fiber
Zucchini, cooked (½ cup)	1.4g soluble fiber	1.2g insoluble fiber

LOOPHOLES AND SNEAKY MATH

Did you notice I included partial grams of fiber (after the decimal point)? I don't normally do that (too much math for this lazy, **keto** lady), but I wanted to see if you were paying attention—*while driving home a point*. Data printed on the US nutrition label does not have decimals.

Macronutrient grams are rounded UP or DOWN to the nearest whole number.

You might be thinking…*so what?* Isn't that against the DIRTY, LAZY, KETO way to obsess over every detail? When it comes to low-carb vegetables, I agree. Point four, rounded down to the nearest carb to calculate the net carbs for a half cup of zucchini isn't going to cause any harm.

None of us became overweight by overeating raw vegetables.

The trouble is when we abuse high-risk ingredients like heavy whipping cream (HWC), the ingredient I call the scarlet letter of DIRTY, LAZY, KETO. I might be dating myself there with *The Scarlet Letter* reference, so maybe I'll reference HBO's *Game of Thrones* instead:

"For shame! For shame! Atone for causing weight loss stalls and even gains I say to you, heavy whipping cream!"

If you look at the nutrition label of HWC, you'll notice…

Nutrition Facts

Serving Size 1 Tbsp (15 mL)
Servings Per Container 32

Amount Per Serving

Calories 52	Calories from Fat 50

	% Daily Value*
Total Fat 5g	**8%**
Saturated Fat 3.5g	**17%**
Trans Fat 0g	
Cholesterol 20mg	**7%**
Sodium 5mg	**0%**
Total Carbohydrate 0g	**0%**
Dietary Fiber 0g	**0%**
Sugars 0g	
Protein 0g	

HWC appears to have 0 grams of net carbs, right? Here is where many folks get in trouble. They immediately think, *LOOPHOLE!* and start ordering hyper-caloric "keto" Starbucks drinks that are brimming with fat-laden cream, all under the guise of losing weight. *Bad idea!* In reality, HWC has 0.4 grams of net carbohydrates per 1 tablespoon serving and has 52 calories. In the United States, nutrition labels are rounded up or down, so the net carbs for HWC falsely *look like zero.* Can you see how quickly the damage of this oversight could add up?

SUGAR ALCOHOLS DON'T COUNT AS CARBS

Besides subtracting fiber, DIRTY, LAZY, KETO recommends subtracting sugar alcohols. Sugar alcohols act like fiber as they aren't fully digested by the body. While some are found naturally inside of fruits/vegetables, others are artificially created. Some contain calories, while others don't. One thing they all have in common, though, is that they TASTE SWEET! Score one for #dirtylazyketo.

Examples of sugar alcohols are:

- Erythritol
- Maltitol
- Sorbitol
- Xylitol

Using sugar alcohols is a personal decision. This topic evokes VERY STRONG opinions in the keto community! DIRTY, LAZY, KETO supports you making your *own* choice, without judgment or criticism. There are no keto police here in DIRTY, LAZY, KETO–land!

> Be aware that not all sugar alcohols are created equal. Everyone reacts differently to sugar alcohols in their body.

You will have to make your own decision about this one! While your body may not have a reaction, here are some of the reported side effects that some folks experience:

- Gastrointestinal distress
- Headache
- Spike in blood sugar (especially with maltitol)
- Craving for more sweet foods

Personally, I feel the benefits of using sugar alcohols outweigh any potential side effects. When faced with having a piece of sugar-free candy or an all-out binge on eating junk food, I choose the former hands down. I feel these decisions have helped me to lose 140 pounds and maintain that weight loss for seven years. Take THAT, keto police—*Bam!*

CHAPTER 2

SAVE TIME AND MONEY

GOOD HEALTH IS *PRICELESS*

I'm sure this all sounds great to you at this point, but deep down, I know you might be worried… How much is this going to cost? Will it take up a lot of time? *Patience, grasshopper.* I'm getting there! Let's address your nagging suspicions right now. I want to share the good news that DIRTY, LAZY, KETO does not have to take over your life! Let's get to the nitty-gritty. With the right meal planning and judicious shopping for ingredients, your grocery bill can actually go down. As an added bonus, because you're efficient at shopping and at home in the kitchen, you'll end up with more free time, not less.

Eating healthy does not have to cost extra. *Really!* In fact, many families report SAVING money as a result of this lifestyle. GONE are the expensive boxes of name-brand cereal, GONE are the pricey chips that go stale in just a few days, and GONE are the shopping carts full of junk food.

> Ultimately, processed, packaged food costs MORE from your pocketbook while stealing *years* off your lifespan.

A healthy body doesn't get sick as often. You'll save money and time avoiding expensive prescriptions, co-pays, and unnecessary doctor visits.

WHEN TO SPEND UP

You don't have to be cheap to save. Ironically, not every tip shared in *The DIRTY, LAZY, KETO® Dirt Cheap Cookbook* is geared toward putting more money in your pocket. Sometimes, it's important to spend! But how? Knowing *when* and *where* to spend your precious dollars is just as important as knowing when to put the credit card away.

Crack Open the Wallet

I might surprise you with this message, but sometimes throwing money at a problem actually WORKS! Let me explain. There are times, in fact, when cracking open your wallet to pay for luxury items can help with weight loss. But when? For what?

> Sometimes, spending more on certain grocery items is worth the extra expense if the payout is keeping you on track.

Let me help you determine when it's acceptable to pay "up" by evaluating the decision using the following "make it or break it" DLK criteria: **Spend more on a grocery item when it helps you with portion control, convenience, and/or compliance.**

I Just Can't Stop!

For me, there are certain foods I tend to overeat. I know in my heart that I should "stop" after eating 1 ounce of my favorite nut, but sometimes I just can't! I keep eating more. I've tried many creative ways to keep myself in check, like using a shot glass to measure out one portion or limiting myself to one handful…but sometimes these strategies *just don't work.* Sure, I could "pre-measure" individual servings into small Ziploc bags. That works sometimes for me, but not always.

There have been times where I've decided that purchasing individually wrapped servings of nuts (like for packing lunches) is my best course of action. True, travel sizes cost more than buying in bulk, but because of my tendency to overeat my favorite nuts, I feel the upsell is worth any added expense.

What foods do you struggle with regarding portion control? Some common answers I hear are low-carb ice cream, nut butter, cheese whisps, pork rinds, string cheese, and sugar-free chocolates. In these instances, I recommend spending more money on portion-controlled sizes (or skip the items completely).

Fighting the Clock—Make It Convenient

If not having enough time is getting in your way of eating heathier, consider investing in a few shortcuts to speed up meal prep. Sure, ricing cauliflower or shredding "zoodles" by hand might save you a few dollars here and there, but what if you're in a hurry? Not everyone has that kind of time to spend in the kitchen. I would rather you buy ready-to-eat veggies than go without. I'm never going to wash heads of lettuce or shred my own broccoli coleslaw mix. Instead, I budget a little extra for these already prepared, time-saving grocery items. For you, what convenience foods are worth spending a little extra money on? Aside from the foods I already mentioned, other popular answers I hear are packaged salads, shredded cheese, and spice mixes.

The Absolutes—I Gotta Have It!

There are certain foods that I just *have to stock* in my fridge. It's like I can't live without them, *no matter what the cost!* For example, I love to eat yogurt for breakfast. If I can't find a low-carb version on sale, do I skip buying yogurt at the grocery store? *No way!* I've been known to spend a king's ransom for a pint of yogurt. This food is important to me, and I'm willing to spend a little extra in order to keep myself on track with DIRTY, LAZY, KETO. I don't feel this way about many foods, so I'm not worried about a couple of extra bucks spent here or there. Eating healthy is a priority for me, and sometimes that means putting my money where my mouth is. *What foods can you not live without?* I'm sure it's a short list.

Allow yourself a little indulgence when compliance is at stake.

Not every food on your grocery list will fall into one of these three categories; in fact, very few should. The trick is to look over your list and identify what's *really important to you*. If your goal is to lose weight on a budget, you must judiciously prioritize where to spend every precious dollar. Occasionally splurging on foods that help with portion control, convenience, or compliance are ironically worth every penny.

WHEN TO SPEND DOWN

A reader reached out to me from North Pole, Alaska (seriously!) asking, "Stephanie, considering where I live, can I eat the right foods for DIRTY, LAZY, KETO?"

Her question is actually quite common. Weather and geography greatly impact the availability of fresh foods to many parts of the world. Despite knowing her remote location, I confidently responded that:

> DIRTY, LAZY, KETO is possible no matter where you live.

If a hard-to-find ingredient was called for in one of my recipes, I offered her the suggestion to swap it out for something similar (or ask Santa for help—*she lives in a place called North Pole, after all!*).

Access to fresh fruits and vegetables might be a challenge where you live too. Whether it's due to your remote location (like our Alaskan friend), or due to higher costs at your supermarket, don't let barriers to fresh foods stop you from eating healthier. There is another way!

The backbone of DIRTY, LAZY, KETO is built upon high-fiber, non-starchy vegetables. When accompanied with healthy fats and a moderate amount of lean protein, they fill you up quickly and help you to feel satisfied for longer amounts of time. For successful, long-lasting weight loss, it's imperative that you build as many vegetables into your daily routine as humanly possible.

> How you buy vegetables (fresh, canned, frozen), in my opinion, doesn't really matter. What's really important is that you eat vegetables!

Stop stressing about trying to buy fresh food all of the time and embrace the lazy portion of DIRTY, LAZY, KETO.

Write this down somewhere: *just do your best*—that's enough!

Frozen Salad? I Don't Think So!

I'm not denying the benefits of fresh produce. Their vibrant color, crisp texture, and seasonal bounty romance me like a holiday Hallmark commercial. Don't laugh, but I love the pressure of trying to eat up the fresh vegetables I buy before they spoil. It's like a vegetable arms race at my house. The clock starts ticking once I come home from the store. The cheap side of my brain won't tolerate a wilting celery stalk going to waste! (You might even recall the No-Guilt Vegetable Soup recipe from *The DIRTY, LAZY, KETO® Cookbook: Bend the Rules to Lose the Weight!* where I resuscitate dying vegetables into a lively dinner.)

Certainly, there are many dishes I will only eat with fresh ingredients. A leafy green salad would NOT make sense coming out of the pantry or freezer. In my opinion, I'd rather eat my lettuce fresh, or not at all. That's the beauty of DIRTY, LAZY, KETO. It's flexible and up to you.

> If you prefer to eat a specific vegetable fresh, then prioritize your dollars to make that happen.

PACKAGED PRODUCE COUNTS

When fresh isn't an option, canned (or jarred) vegetables offer many unique advantages. They don't expire like fresh food and are available year-round. They don't take up much room either. I love catching a good sale—because canned goods are so affordable, I stock my pantry with DIRTY, LAZY, KETO favorites for a rainy day. Yes, I'm sure canned goods are heavily processed and contain added salt. No one is arguing with you there! But in my opinion, the benefits of eating canned vegetables (versus eating none at all) outweigh any negatives. Convenience and affordability matter more to me than quality.

I am willing to sacrifice the texture and color of my vegetables if it means I am able to build a healthy meal in lieu of binge eating tortilla chips.

If you were to look inside my pantry right now, you'd find it stocked with various canned (or jarred) vegetables and related vegetable products such as:

- Asparagus
- Black olives
- Green beans
- Green chiles
- Green olives
- Green salsa
- Hearts of palm
- Hunt's Pasta Sauce (no-sugar-added)
- Jalapeños
- Mushrooms
- Pickles
- Pumpkin (100% pure)
- Rao's Homemade Marinara Sauce
- Sun-dried tomatoes in oil
- Tomatillos

Like having a multitude of canned vegetables in your pantry, stocking your freezer with low-carb vegetables guarantees you have healthier options. Frozen foods will last forever. Yes, the texture or flavor of frozen vegetables might differ from fresh, but the technology of frozen foods has come a long way. Frozen vegetables are picked at the peak of harvest and flash frozen with minimal processing. Don't be afraid to stock your freezer with low-carb, affordable options.

Here's a sneak peek at the buried treasures in my freezer:

- Broccoli florets
- Brussels sprouts
- Edamame
- Fajita bell pepper mix
- Green beans
- Riced cauliflower

- Spinach
- Zucchini squash
- Zucchini "zoodles"

> Don't let the perfect be the enemy of the good. Having an assortment of canned, jarred, and frozen vegetables on hand will provide excellent nutrition along with peace of mind. Don't let access to fresh foods become an excuse for not eating healthy.

Now that your kitchen is stocked with healthy ingredients, it's time to put that produce to work. When you have a fridge and pantry full of food, the only thing stopping you from cooking is deciding what to make. I can help with that!

AVOID THE DREADED "WHAT'S FOR DINNER?"

Any time you spend planning meals is worth its weight in gold. Not only will you waste less money on uneaten groceries or restaurant bills, but you will gain confidence in your ability to succeed. I can't begin to tell you how much time in my life I have wasted thinking about "what's for dinner?" This question really stresses me out! I don't want to get halfway through making a recipe before discovering I lack crucial ingredients. Even worse, I want to avoid impulsively eating a bunch of junk just because I'm STARVING and there is nothing available for me to eat.

> Having a plan puts you back in control.

Even with the DIRTY, LAZY, KETO grocery list and 100 affordable recipes at your disposal, there is still the matter of your precious time. I know you're busy! Even the most dedicated chef gets tired of making dinner every single day of the week. There is no sense burning yourself out. This is Lazy Keto, after all! Sometimes it's more important to catch up on *Netflix*, take a walk, or spend time with your family than to stand over a hot stove. I've got a solution for those days.

Sure, your first thought might be to drive to a restaurant or have takeout food delivered. Throwing money at the problem is always our gut reaction to saving time. But what if there was another way? The answer is right in front of you: *leftovers!* (That was SOOOOOO not what you were expecting, *right?*)

LEFTOVERS IN DISGUISE

When you go to all the trouble of making a delicious DIRTY, LAZY, KETO recipe, I recommend making enough to last a few days. Go ahead and double the recipe! Before you go "poo-pooing" leftovers, hear me out.

> Cooking in bulk saves time and money, the two things we can never seem to have enough of!

DIRTY, LAZY, KETO recipes are so good that my family fights over the leftovers. Please don't tell Bill (my coauthor and husband) that I often hide servings from our favorite DIRTY, LAZY, KETO recipes. I've been known to strategically push the Tupperware toward the back of the fridge while camouflaging its positioning with wilted vegetables. I'm being stealth, you see, like hiding Halloween candy inside an empty plastic vegetable bag at the bottom of the freezer. (No one ever checks there!) Leftovers at my house are in high demand and intensely fought over. We are a family of frequent snackers. By hiding the Tupperware of leftovers, I'm ensuring there will be enough for dinner tonight, so please don't judge.

If leftovers aren't your jam, I have another creative idea for you to try. It's kind of a Texas two-step dance in the kitchen. I call it the *dinner reboot.* As I mentioned in *The DIRTY, LAZY, KETO® Cookbook: Bend the Rules to Lose the Weight!*, I often reinvent dinner for multiple days in a row. Even the pickiest eaters in my family haven't caught on to my magic trick! Tuesday's tacos magically morph into a casserole the next day. No one in my family has ever complained. Because a portion of the first meal is reinvented for the second dinner, you will stretch your dollar, reduce your time in the kitchen, and avoid exasperation deciding "what's for dinner?" (which is priceless). Throughout this book, recipes worthy of rebooting are designated with the handy-dandy icon: ↻

Suggestions on how to reinvent a meal or revive a hefty part of its ingredients are explained in the recipe's designated Tips and

Options section. Think of reboot recipes as sisters. *Ta-da!* More time saved. No flipping around with sticky fingers trying to figure out what to do. *You're welcome.*

WRAP IT UP! FOOD SAFETY

To alleviate any lingering concerns you might have about the safety of leftovers, let's take a deep dive into food storage safety tips. According to the USDA, as long as you prepare and refrigerate food according to recommended guidelines, you can continue to enjoy leftovers for three to four days. That's going to save you a lot of time and money!

Follow these guidelines to stay healthy and enjoy leftovers.

1   **Cook food thoroughly.** Verify completion using a food thermometer while it's still cooking.
    - Red meat (minimum internal temperature of 145°F)
    - Ground meat (minimum internal temperature of 160°F)
    - Poultry (minimum internal temperature of 165°F)
2   **Keep hot food hot, and cold food cold.**
    - Hot means 140°F or warmer
    - Cold means 40°F or colder
3   **Eat it or store it.** The maximum amount of time food should be left out (room temperature) is 2 hours.
4   **Break it up.** When it's time to refrigerate food, cool it faster by dividing it into smaller portions.
5   *Tight, tight, tight!* Store any leftovers using Ziploc bags, airtight plastic wrap, and/or properly fitting lids. This helps keep food fresh and prevent bacteria from growing.
6   **Chill out.** The safest way to thaw frozen meat is in the refrigerator. Otherwise, you can wrap frozen meat using airtight packaging and submerge in cold water. In a hurry? The fastest way to thaw meat is by using the microwave.
7   **Temperature matters!** When you reheat your leftovers, be sure the internal temperature reaches a minimum of 165°F or higher.
8   **Super-thrifty?** You can make leftovers of your leftovers! Freeze and reheat using provided recommendations.

9 **When in doubt, throw it out.** If something doesn't look right or smell right, trust your instincts and get rid of it. Your health and safety are the number one priority.

STEPHANIE'S "DIRT CHEAP" TRICKS TO SAVE MONEY AND TIME

None of this theory matters if you don't apply it in the kitchen. Prioritizing your resources doesn't have to be complicated. Following are ten specific examples that show how I budget time and money within my own household. I encourage you to steal, modify, and add to this list of ideas. *Customize DLK to work for you!*

1 **Easy peasy.** I use time-saving and convenient kitchen gadgets like the Instant Pot®, slow cooker, or air fryer to do all the work for me. I minimize the number of dishes for cooking at all costs!

2 **It's a date.** I schedule shopping trips on the same day/time each week. Knowing when food will be purchased reduces unnecessary anxiety over having the right ingredients on hand.

3 **Make-ahead Monday.** I plan multiple meals at a time that share common ingredients. For example, cauliflower rice made on Monday can be added to soup on Tuesday, and so on. I wash and cut vegetables early in the week to enjoy throughout the week.

4 **Weekly holidays.** Taco Tuesday, Meatless Monday, Soup Sunday… Traditions eliminate the guesswork of what to eat for dinner that night. Scheduling themed meals holds me accountable to myself and my family. Plus, it's fun; olé!

5 **Instant happiness!** Sometimes, I treat myself. When I'm pressed for time, I eliminate potential barriers to healthy eating and buy already prepped vegetables sold in ready-to-eat (or cook) packaging.

6 **Ask for help.** I often enlist (assign? bribe?) family members to participate with meal prep, freeing up my time while encouraging others to learn a new skill.

7 **Double or nothing.** I make double what a recipe calls for and freeze/enjoy it another day.

8 **Day off.** I plan ahead for a specific night off from the kitchen. Knowing I don't have to cook on Saturday, for example, helps keep me motivated to prep and cook the rest of the week.

9 **Packaged veggies.** I let go of trying to be perfect. I realize that actually eating veggies is what matters to me—not whether they are fresh, frozen, canned, or jarred.

10 **Plan for "me time."** I take care of myself outside of the kitchen. Self-care makes me feel nourished in ways that eating never can.

Planning for the week's meals and sticking to a strategic shopping list can be your best friend when on a budget. Eating healthy doesn't have to be expensive. By utilizing these steps, you'll end up saving, not spending extra money. Planning your meals leads to successful weight loss. You'll look and feel fabulous. And that, my friends, *is priceless.*

CHAPTER 3

GROCERY SHOPPING

STRATEGY AND MINDSET

There is no need to aimlessly walk around the grocery store trying to figure out what to buy. Your time is valuable, so let's get in and out quickly without spending unnecessary wads of cash. I don't know about you, but the more time I spend in a store, the more I tend to buy! I'm sure that's why the aisles in stores are designed to be so long. It's like they're trying to trap you! When I'm surrounded by 6-foot walls of convenience foods, I lose all perspective and add unnecessary items to my cart. Let's prevent that from happening! I'm going to spill my tips for time management, direct you where to shop, and suggest how to save money by planning and selecting ingredients. Let's get started!

Before we head to the store, here are ten specific money- and time-saving strategies I'd like you to think about to put you in the right frame of mind:

1 **YOU go to the store.** You can't blame other people for not buying the proper DLK-friendly foods or forgetting to be frugal. That's scapegoating, not shopping.
2 **Avoid all food that says "KETO" on it.** It's probably expensive and unnecessary.
3 **Decide now that you're going to eat real food!** Shop the outside perimeter of the grocery store where fresh meats, vegetables, fruits, and dairy are usually located.

4   **Go to the store often.** I go twice a week. Really! If you go on a regular schedule to buy fresh foods, you tend to buy only what you need, reducing waste.

5   **Buy meats in bulk when you catch a good sale.** Stock up your freezer or split an order with a friend/family member.

6   **Be open-minded about ways to save.** Canned or frozen vegetables, for example, might be an opportunity to save money.

7   **Avoid buying specialty baking items at your regular grocery store,** where items can be pricey. (Think $10.99 for a bag of almond flour! No thanks.) Instead, check out discount retail stores and stock up.

8   **Don't be afraid to buy fresh veggies.** If you aren't sure when you'll be able to use your fresh vegetables, and this is making you nervous about buying them, remember there are other ways to "extend their life" (like steaming or boiling them followed by refrigeration).

9   **Stock up on sale items.** Buy multiple bags of sale items you use regularly (like shredded cheese) to freeze for future use.

10 **Make your own.** If you tend to use a pricey ingredient, like Carbquik or Trader Joe's Everything but the Bagel Sesame Seasoning Blend, assemble your own version using bulk ingredients.

FIND THE BEST DEALS

Now that your mind is on the right track, you are ready to head to the store. Where should you go first? It's a common misconception that your local grocery chain offers the best prices. For some items, yes, but not overall! To make a significant dent in your grocery budget, you must shop at a variety of stores. Sure, this takes a bit more effort, but with the right strategy in place, it's time well spent.

In my experience, targeting multiple grocery stores for the sole purpose of purchasing their loss leaders is worth the time and energy. A loss leader is an item the store sells as close to, or even below, the wholesale cost. Basically, the store isn't making much (if any) profit on the item, taking a "loss." Why on Earth would a store opt-in for this type of strategy? Because it works! Sure, shoppers seek out stores with heavily discounted items to purchase, but they then start filling up their grocery cart with items that are NOT on sale. Therein lies the profit model of loss leaders.

In order to take advantage of this financial *puka*—the Hawaiian word for "hole"—you have to stay savvy to playing the game. I'm not suggesting you become a crazy coupon lady with shelves of deodorant stocked in your basement; rather, just pay attention to your local stores selling keto foods at competitive prices. That's all.

Saving money doesn't have to be a hassle. When the dollars add up, thriftiness becomes even more rewarding. Instead of thinking the extra trips to grocery stores are a hassle, reframe the extra stops like a game: a DIRTY, LAZY, KETO scavenger hunt! Saving money is motivating. Just think, you'll need all that extra cash to buy new clothes because you lost so much weight!

Grocery prices fluctuate. Weather, location, seasons, and competition affect the price of goods. With these considerations in mind, I'd like to offer you *a general idea* of the types of stores likely to offer the lowest prices on a given keto item. (Note that some grocery items will repeat under multiple headings when appropriate.) I understand you may not have access to all the stores on this list. Every community is different. Plus, many items discussed here are luxury or boutique keto foods. You can certainly lose weight without enjoying a $2 mini bag of Quest chips, that's for sure! I am just trying to pass on my knowledge about where to find the best prices, should you opt for a special treat.

Superstores
- Bacon
- Bouillon cubes
- Butter
- Canned goods
- Chicken (rotisserie)
- Chocolate chips (sugar-free)
- Deli meat
- Eggs
- "Everything but the Bagel" seasoning
- Hot cocoa mix (packaged, single-serving, nonfat)
- Jams, jellies, and preserves (sugar-free)
- Meat (fresh)

- Meat (frozen)
- Milk (unsweetened dairy alternative milk like almond, cashew, coconut, hemp, or soy)
- Pancake syrup (sugar-free)
- Pickles
- Sauces (in can or jar)
- Spice blends (packaged taco powder, au jus gravy powder, ranch powder, and so on)
- Tortillas (low-carb)
- Vegetables (canned)
- Vegetables (frozen)
- Yogurt (full-fat, plain, Greek-style)

Warehouse or Wholesale Club Stores
- Almond flour (superfine)
- Cauliflower (frozen, riced)
- Cheese (shredded)
- Chicken (rotisserie)
- Marinara sauce (Rao's Homemade)
- Nuts
- Oil
- Pesto sauce
- Protein bars (Quest, Kirkland)

Neighborhood Grocery Stores
- Cream (full-fat heavy whipping cream)
- Diet soda
- Electrolyte water (sugar-free)
- Gelatin powder (sugar-free)
- Ice cream (low-carb; Rebel, Enlightened, store brand)
- Mayonnaise (full-fat)
- Mustard
- Salad dressing
- Seafood (fresh)
- Seltzer water (sugar-free)
- Sports drink (sugar-free)
- Yogurt (full-fat, plain, Greek-style)

Boutique Grocery Stores

- Bread (low-carb)
- Candy (sugar-free)
- Chocolate (unsweetened baking, 100% cacao)
- Chocolate bar (85%–92% cacao)
- "Everything but the Bagel" seasoning
- Fish (fresh)
- Jams, jellies, and preserves (sugar-free)
- Nut butter or no-sugar-added peanut butter
- Olives

Discount Grocery Stores

- Candy (hard, sugar-free)
- Coconut milk, canned (unsweetened, 12%–14% fat)
- Gum (sugar-free)
- Hot dogs
- Hot sauce
- Marinara sauce (no-sugar-added; Heinz)
- Pork rinds
- Water flavor packets and squirts

Ethnic Grocery Stores

- Coconut milk, canned (unsweetened, 12%–14% fat)
- Fruit (fresh)
- Herbs (fresh)
- Hot sauce
- Meat (fresh, pre-spiced)
- Sauce starters
- Spices (ethnic)
- Vegetables (fresh)

"Closeout" Discount Stores

- Baking products (low-carb, example: Bob's Red Mill)
- Gourmet coffee and tea
- Sugar substitutes
- Syrup (flavored, sugar-free, brands like Torani, DaVinci, or Jordan's Skinny Syrups)
- Upscale or unique cooking oils (high-quality olive oil, truffle oil, flavored infused oils)

Farmers' Markets and Co-ops

- Fruit (fresh, in season)
- Herbs (fresh, in season)
- Homemade specialty items (sauces, salsa, pesto, and so on)
- Vegetables (fresh, in season)

Neighborhood Pharmacy*

- Beer (low-carb)
- Liquor (unflavored hard alcohol)
- Malt beverage (low-carb)
- Wine (dry)

If permitted to sell alcohol by state liquor law.

Online

Ordering direct from retailers often provides unseen benefits like discounts for bulk purchasing, free delivery, and immediate access to hard-to-find varieties.

- Barbecue sauce (sugar-free)
- Black soybeans
- Carbquik baking powder
- Chia seeds
- Flax meal
- Flaxseed
- Flour substitutes
- Ice cream (low-carb, brands like Enlightened)
- MCT oil
- Oil for cooking
- Sugar substitutes
- Syrup (flavored, sugar-free, brands like Torani, DaVinci, or Jordan's Skinny Syrups)

GROCERY LIST FOR DIRTY, LAZY, KETO

Now that you know where to shop for the best prices, I'll provide you with a quick beginner DIRTY, LAZY, KETO grocery list for your first time at the store. No sense getting overwhelmed before you even start! These groceries are my staples. I'm sure your favorites might be different. Add items from your planned recipes as needed.

Drinks (all sugar-free)
- ❏ Coffee, unsweetened
- ❏ Diet soda
- ❏ Energy drinks
- ❏ Flavor packets (or squirts) to add to water
- ❏ Sports drinks with electrolytes
- ❏ Tea, unsweetened (herbal, black)
- ❏ Water (plain, sparkling, flavored)

Meats (without sugar additives)
- ❏ Bacon
- ❏ Deli meat
- ❏ Protein: beef, pork, poultry, seafood, soy foods, soy protein isolates (mock meat)
- ❏ Sausage

Dairy
- ❏ Butter
- ❏ Cheese (all kinds, full-fat)
- ❏ Eggs
- ❏ Half and half (full-fat)
- ❏ Heavy whipping cream
- ❏ Milk (dairy alternative milk like almond milk, unsweetened)
- ❏ Sour cream (full-fat)
- ❏ Yogurt (full-fat, plain, Greek-style)

Produce

- ❏ Avocados
- ❏ Broccoli
- ❏ Cabbage
- ❏ Cauliflower
- ❏ Celery
- ❏ Salad mix
- ❏ Vegetables (low-carb, your choice)

Miscellaneous

- ❏ Candy (sugar-free)
- ❏ Flavored gelatin (sugar-free)
- ❏ Mayonnaise (full-fat)
- ❏ Nut butter (no-sugar-added)
- ❏ Oil
- ❏ Olives
- ❏ Pickles
- ❏ Salad dressing (suggestion: ranch or blue cheese)
- ❏ Tortillas (low-carb)

For more help picking out the right groceries, visit the DIRTY, LAZY, KETO YouTube channel at: https://youtube.com/c/ DIRTYLAZYKETOStephanieLaska

THE DIRTY, LAZY, KETO RECIPES

They Only Taste Expensive

CHAPTER 4

BREAKFAST

I'm going to tell you something really embarrassing. On days where I don't want to get out of bed, thinking about breakfast is often what gets me moving! I love to eat *that much*.

When I was a kid, breakfast usually consisted of some kind of sugary cereal. **If it didn't come with a prize in the box, I wasn't interested.** To this day, I can visualize the brightly colored boxes all lined up in my childhood pantry. My brother and I would fight over the last pour of Fruity Pebbles—that box was always just a little bit smaller than the others, and therefore more coveted. We would eat bowl after bowl of this sugary deliciousness while watching morning cartoons, washing it all down by slurping the leftover pink milk directly from the bowl.

When I was away from home, like at a sleepover, I got to witness what other families ate for breakfast. I was astonished to find so many friends eating generic, plain corn flakes. *Plain*, as in no sugar; *Eh!* How did those people *survive?* It felt like prison. Adding spoonful after spoonful of table sugar didn't help the situation either. The grains just sank to the bottom of the bowl like sand in a fishbowl.

Clearly, breakfast is important to me. From a very young age, I've been conditioned to expect something sweet first thing in the morning. As an adult, this habit was hard (if not impossible!) to change. I've learned to work with, not against, my tendency to prefer morning sweets. Instead of empty carbohydrates, however, I now enjoy a sugar-free alternative. From **chaffles** to muffins, here are my DIRTY, LAZY, KETO breakfast favorites.

CLOSEOUT COCOA PUFFS CHAFFLE

✗ ◉ 🌿 ✦

Growing up in the 70s, one of my favorite breakfast cereals was Cocoa Puffs. I would overfill my bowl with milk knowing the cereal would create a secondary treat: chocolate-flavored milk! My brother and I would race to refill our bowls of cereal. Whoever emptied the box first got to keep the free toy at the bottom. Between the two of us, let's just say I won a lot of prizes! Nowadays, I avoid the cereal aisle altogether. *Too many carbs!* I miss the fun flavors, though. That's what motivated me to create the Closeout Cocoa Puffs Chaffle.

5 large eggs, beaten

4 tablespoons soy flour

3 tablespoons low-carb protein powder

2 tablespoons 100% cocoa powder

2 tablespoons unsweetened vanilla almond milk

2 tablespoons pure vanilla extract

4 tablespoons heavy whipping cream

6 tablespoons 0g net carbs sweetener

3 tablespoons sugar-free chocolate chips

1   Spray a waffle iron with nonstick cooking spray. Preheat waffle iron.

2   Add all ingredients (except chocolate chips) to a blender. Pulse 30 seconds, stopping to scrape the sides. Pulse 30 seconds more.

3   Add chocolate chips to blender. Pulse for only a few seconds.

4   Immediately pour ¼ cup batter onto each waffle pattern, making two chaffles at a time. Be careful not to overfill. Close waffle iron. Cook 3 minutes.

5   Use a plastic fork to gently remove chaffles from iron. Repeat steps until all the batter is gone.

6   Serve immediately.

LAST CHANCE CHOCOLATE CHIP CHAFFLE

✗ ◉ 🍃 ✦

TOTAL COST $4.10
COST PER SERVING $1.03

NET CARBS

3G

SERVES 4

PER SERVING:

CALORIES	194
FAT	14G
PROTEIN	11G
SODIUM	211MG
FIBER	3G
CARBOHYDRATES	7G
NET CARBS	3G
SUGAR	1G
SUGAR ALCOHOL	1.5G

TIME

PREP TIME:	5 MINUTES
COOK TIME:	20 MINUTES

TIPS & OPTIONS »

I recommend using a plastic fork to gently pry finished chaffles from the iron. A plastic fork won't scratch or damage its Teflon surface.

If you're having a Last Chance Chocolate Chip Chaffle for dessert, top with a serving of *frozen* Cool Whip. (Not lite! The regular flavor of Cool Whip is lowest in net carbs.) Frozen Cool Whip tastes like ice cream. *No joke!*

Are Last Chance Chocolate Chip Chaffles eaten only at breakfast? NOPE! This recipe calls my name *all...day...long*! Let's have a serious conversation for a moment. Here lies the problem with **chaffles** (which originated as plain cheese waffles in case you forgot). They are so tasty that I could *seriously* eat a dozen chaffles at a time! A+ for *carboliciousness*! Because I'm portion-control challenged, I have to limit myself to enjoying chaffles of any nature on *Sundays* only.

> **2 large eggs**
> **1 cup shredded whole milk mozzarella**
> **¼ cup superfine blanched almond flour**
> **½ tablespoon pure vanilla extract**
> **5 (1-gram) packets 0g net carbs sweetener**
> **2 tablespoons sugar-free chocolate chips**

1. Spray a mini waffle maker with nonstick cooking spray and turn waffle maker on to preheat.

2. Combine all ingredients in a medium mixing bowl.

3. Once waffle maker has warmed, add ¼ of batter. Close waffle maker and cook 4–5 minutes until fully cooked.

4. Use a plastic fork to gently remove chaffle from iron. Repeat until all the batter is gone.

5. Serve warm.

SWEET HOME SAVINGS CINNAMON CHAFFLE

✗ ◉ 🌿 ★

Chaffles again? *It must be Sunday at my house!* I take my chaffles seriously. Normally I don't recommend buying a bunch of "one-timer" kitchen tools, but investing in a waffle iron should be an exception. Chaffle iron, waffle iron…they all work the same. My grandmother used the same waffle iron for like, fifty years. Aside from the frayed cord looking like a fire hazard, her iron worked just as well as my new Black Friday special.

½ cup superfine blanched almond flour

1 tablespoon 0g net carbs sweetener

½ teaspoon baking powder

¼ teaspoon ground cinnamon

⅛ teaspoon salt

2 medium eggs

½ teaspoon pure vanilla extract

3 tablespoons unsalted butter, melted

1. Spray a large waffle iron with nonstick cooking spray and preheat.

2. In a blender, mix all ingredients for 30 seconds. Scrape sides with spatula and blend again for 30 seconds.

3. Pour ⅓ of mixture onto each waffle iron pattern. Close waffle iron and cook 3 minutes.

4. Use a plastic fork to gently remove chaffles from iron. Repeat steps until all the batter is gone.

5. Serve warm.

TOTAL COST	$4.66
COST PER SERVING	$1.17

NET CARBS

1G

SERVES 4

PER SERVING:

CALORIES	204
FAT	17G
PROTEIN	6G
SODIUM	322MG
FIBER	2G
CARBOHYDRATES	5G
NET CARBS	1G
SUGAR	1G
SUGAR ALCOHOL	1.6G

TIME

PREP TIME:	10 MINUTES
COOK TIME:	10 MINUTES

⟪ TIPS & OPTIONS

Even though waffle irons have a nonstick surface, I spray the iron with nonstick cooking spray prior to heating it up. Chaffles can get sticky! I do everything I can to help ease them from the mold.

Top with sugar-free pancake syrup. Two of my favorite brands are Mrs. Butterworth's Sugar Free Syrup and Lakanto's Maple Flavored Syrup. Delicious!

Always pour batter in the middle of the waffle iron as it quickly disperses when the lid is closed.

Clean your waffle iron by wiping with a damp cloth.

SOS BOND BISCUITS AND GRAVY

My husband's family is hard-core military. He grew up on base and later served in the armed forces himself. This lifetime of experience instilled no-nonsense beliefs about eating breakfast. *No whining! No special orders!* Eat your ration of SOS and exit the mess hall in a timely fashion says Captain Laska. *Woo-ah!*

Biscuits

1¼ cups superfine blanched almond flour

1 teaspoon 0g net carbs sweetener

2 teaspoons baking powder

½ teaspoon baking soda

⅛ teaspoon salt

2 large eggs

3 ounces full-fat cream cheese, softened

3 tablespoons unsalted butter, softened

⅓ cup shredded Cheddar cheese

Gravy

½ pound loose breakfast sausage, cooked

4 tablespoons heavy whipping cream

2 tablespoons full-fat cream cheese, softened

⅛ teaspoon garlic powder

⅛ teaspoon salt

⅛ teaspoon black pepper

1 Preheat oven to 425°F. Grease eight cups of a muffin tin.

2 In a medium mixing bowl, combine almond flour, sweetener, baking powder, baking soda, and salt.

3 In a separate medium mixing bowl, combine eggs, cream cheese, butter, and Cheddar cheese.

4 Whisk dry ingredients into egg mixture until thoroughly mixed. Add batter evenly to eight muffin cups.

5 Bake 13–15 minutes until starting to brown.

6 In a medium saucepan over medium heat, add all the gravy ingredients and stir to combine. Heat 5 minutes, stirring until cream cheese is melted and combined.

7 Serve each biscuit with 2 tablespoons gravy.

| TOTAL COST | $7.69 |
| COST PER SERVING | $0.96 |

NET CARBS

3G

SERVES 8

PER SERVING:

CALORIES	374
FAT	32G
PROTEIN	11G
SODIUM	605MG
FIBER	2G
CARBOHYDRATES	5G
NET CARBS	3G
SUGAR	2G
SUGAR ALCOHOL	0.3G

TIME

| PREP TIME: | 10 MINUTES |
| COOK TIME: | 20 MINUTES |

TIPS & OPTIONS

There are no variations in the military. You get what you get and you don't throw a fit!

Make extra portions of the gravy here and reboot for Down Payment Da Loco Moco (see recipe in this chapter).

SWEEPSTAKE CHAFFLE ON THE BEACH

TOTAL COST $7.04
COST PER SERVING $1.17

NET CARBS

3G

SERVES 6

PER SERVING:

CALORIES	243
FAT	16G
PROTEIN	14G
SODIUM	110MG
FIBER	4G
CARBOHYDRATES	13G
NET CARBS	3G
SUGAR	3G
SUGAR ALCOHOL	6G

TIME

PREP TIME:	5 MINUTES
COOK TIME:	9 MINUTES

TIPS & OPTIONS »

Resist the temptation to overfill your waffle iron. Pour chaffle batter in the center of each waffle pattern. When the lid closes, the batter will disperse evenly.

Enjoy Sweepstake Chaffle on the Beach with melted butter and sugar-free pancake syrup.

Freeze extra servings of Sweepstake Chaffle on the Beach in Ziploc bags.

Go all in to create a vacation experience. Add a splash of coconut flavored sugar-free syrup to your coffee (I suggest Torani brand).

Do you know what cures post-vacation depression? Planning another vacation! My family makes fun of me for being so travel-obsessed. While some people read magazines to relax, I shop discount travel sites and enter contests. It's true! In between taking actual trips, I take mental vacations by cooking meals using spices bought on past adventures. Enjoying the tropical flavors like these from Hawaii makes me feel like I'm still on vacation.

5 large eggs, beaten

4 tablespoons coconut flour

3 tablespoons low-carb protein powder

½ cup shredded unsweetened coconut

2 tablespoons unsweetened vanilla almond milk

2 tablespoons pure vanilla extract

4 tablespoons heavy whipping cream

6 tablespoons 0g net carbs sweetener

¼ cup chopped macadamia nuts

1   Spray a waffle iron with nonstick cooking spray. Preheat waffle iron.

2   Add all ingredients except nuts to a blender. Pulse 30 seconds, stopping to scrape sides. Pulse 30 seconds more.

3   Add nuts to blender. Pulse for only a few seconds.

4   Immediately pour ¼ cup batter onto each waffle pattern, making two waffles at a time. Be careful not to overfill. Close waffle iron. Cook 3 minutes.

5   Use a plastic fork to gently remove chaffles from iron. Repeat steps until all the batter is gone.

6   Serve immediately.

GIVEAWAY GREEN EGGS AND SPAM

When my kids are being spoiled at Grandma's house, they eat Pop-Tarts or bowls of Frosted Flakes for breakfast. (*Sorry to throw you under the bus, Mom!*) In my kitchen, ironically, I don't force healthy eating on anyone. Instead, I'm trying to lead by example by choosing to eat a hearty breakfast. My usual routine is to eat full-fat yogurt or eggs during the workweek, saving the more complicated (or messy) recipes for the weekend. Giveaway Green Eggs and SPAM is silly, yet easy to make. My kids (and I!) are suckers for oddball food.

1 cup chopped fresh spinach

¾ cup chopped fresh parsley

¼ cup grated Parmesan cheese

⅓ cup olive oil

5 large eggs

⅛ teaspoon salt

⅛ teaspoon black pepper

½ tablespoon unsalted butter

1 (12-ounce) can SPAM Classic, sliced

1. In a food processor, pulse spinach, parsley, cheese, and oil until chopped almost to purée.

2. In a large bowl, whisk eggs and then fold in green sauce, salt, and pepper.

3. In a large skillet over medium heat, melt butter. Stir in egg mixture and continue stirring every few minutes for 12–15 minutes until eggs are cooked. Remove from heat and cover.

4. In a medium skillet over medium heat, brown SPAM 2–3 minutes, flipping at halfway point.

5. Place eggs and SPAM on a plate and serve warm.

TOTAL COST	$4.43
COST PER SERVING	$1.10

NET CARBS

3G

SERVES 4

PER SERVING:	
CALORIES	550
FAT	48G
PROTEIN	22G
SODIUM	1,422MG
FIBER	1G
CARBOHYDRATES	4G
NET CARBS	3G
SUGAR	0G

TIME

PREP TIME:	10 MINUTES
COOK TIME:	18 MINUTES

TIPS & OPTIONS

Enjoy with a hot cup of DLK Bulletproof Coffee (from *The DIRTY, LAZY, KETO® Cookbook*) or Lotto Chai Latte (see Chapter 10) and you'll be full until lunch!

If you are trying out intermittent fasting (IF), postpone this hearty meal for a little later in the day. IF doesn't have to be complicated—for me, it just means not eating after dinner until breakfast the next day.

Not a fan of SPAM? Substitute sliced ham instead.

DOWN PAYMENT DA LOCO MOCO

TOTAL COST — $2.36
COST PER SERVING — $2.36

NET CARBS

4G

SERVES 1

PER SERVING:
CALORIES	173
FAT	9G
PROTEIN	16G
SODIUM	261MG
FIBER	2G
CARBOHYDRATES	6G
NET CARBS	4G
SUGAR	2G

TIME

PREP TIME:	5 MINUTES
COOK TIME:	21 MINUTES
	30 SECONDS

TIPS & OPTIONS »

Play relaxing tiki music while eating Down Payment Da Loco Moco to fully experience Hawaiian comfort food. Legend has it that the Loco Moco was created prewar in Hilo, Hawaii (that's on the Big Island).

Instead of using gravy from a jar, reboot extra gravy created from the SOS Bond Biscuits and Gravy recipe in this chapter.

Make lunch while cooking breakfast. Cook an extra hamburger patty to use inside a lettuce wrap later. With mayo, cheese, onions, and pickles, you can enjoy fast food at home!

With the popularity of intermittent fasting rising, no one seems to care about eating breakfast anymore. Well…maybe everyone except ME! Sometimes eating breakfast is what pulls me out of bed in the morning. I love to eat, and I can't wait to get started. I take breakfast seriously, sometimes enjoying a *second* breakfast mid-morning. I consider it a down payment to prevent overeating later that day. I'm *loco* like that!

1 cup riced cauliflower

1 beef hamburger patty

1 large egg

2 tablespoons premade beef gravy

1 In a medium microwave-safe bowl, microwave cauliflower for 3–4 minutes, let cool. Put cooled cauliflower in colander, place piece of parchment paper directly on top of cauliflower and push down to remove excess water.

2 In a small skillet over medium heat, cook beef patty 10–12 minutes, flipping after 5 minutes. Transfer cooked patty to a plate.

3 In a separate small skillet over medium heat, fry the egg 3–5 minutes.

4 Pour gravy into a small microwave-safe dish. Cover and heat 15–30 seconds.

5 Place cauliflower in a medium bowl. Drizzle with warmed gravy. Stack patty on top of cauliflower. Top patty with fried egg. Serve.

FRUGAL FINAL EXAM YOGURT

I was terrified of my Instant Pot® at first, I'll admit. It looked like a time machine that might explode at any minute. It sat in the box on my counter, with the Christmas wrapping paper still stuck to the sides, *for months*. Eventually, I got tired of wiping up spills around the box and forced myself to watch some how-to videos on *YouTube*. Surprisingly, it wasn't that complicated! I have grown to love this machine more than any other gadget in my kitchen. It's been an adventure figuring out how to use the many features! Learning how to make homemade yogurt in the pressure cooker was my final exam.

4 cups whole milk

⅓ cup full-fat plain Greek yogurt (must have "live active cultures" in list of ingredients)

1   In a covered medium stockpot over medium heat, bring milk to boil; this will take about 5 minutes. Immediately remove from heat and let cool to approximately 115°F, the best fermentation temperature, about 30 minutes; keep covered. Milk that's too hot may kill your live cultures.

2   Add milk and yogurt to Instant Pot® and stir until combined. Close lid, close vent, choose "yogurt" setting, and select 8 hours.

3   Remove from Instant Pot® and chill in refrigerator covered with plastic wrap.

4   Serve chilled.

* Does not include 30 minutes cooling time.

** Does not include 8 hours fermentation time.

EARLY BIRD EGG FOLD

TOTAL COST $3.38
COST PER SERVING $1.69

NET CARBS

4G

SERVES 2

PER SERVING:

CALORIES	628
FAT	48G
PROTEIN	34G
SODIUM	1,185MG
FIBER	1G
CARBOHYDRATES	5G
NET CARBS	4G
SUGAR	2G

TIME

PREP TIME:	10 MINUTES
COOK TIME:	34 MINUTES

I will never tire of eating eggs. They give me such a strong start to the day! I find that eating "heartier" foods (like an omelet) earlier in the morning keeps me feeling fuller for longer periods of time. Omelets, in particular, are forgiving too, perfect for a frugal chef. I can add all sorts of sad-looking, wilted vegetables and/or leftover protein to my skillet. Appearances don't matter here since the ingredients simply disappear inside. As a protein choice, eggs are affordable; omelets make regular appearances in my menu planning, for breakfast *and* dinner!

¼ pound loose pork chorizo

4 large eggs

½ cup chopped fresh spinach

¼ cup chopped white onion

½ small jalapeño pepper, seeded, deveined, and finely chopped

¼ cup heavy whipping cream

½ cup shredded Cheddar cheese, divided

⅛ teaspoon salt, divided

⅛ teaspoon black pepper, divided

1. In a medium skillet over medium heat, brown chorizo 7–10 minutes while stirring. Drain fat, and transfer meat to a medium bowl.

2. In a second medium mixing bowl, whisk eggs, spinach, onion, jalapeño, and cream.

3. Add half of egg mixture to a large nonstick skillet over medium heat. Let cook 5–7 minutes without stirring until bottom has firmed.

4. Add half of the meat evenly to one side and fold in half. Cover and let cook completely 3–5 minutes.

5. Using a silicone spatula, delicately "pour" hot omelet onto plate. Top with half of the cheese, salt, and pepper.

6. Repeat for second omelet. Serve.

TIPS & OPTIONS

Suggested toppings are sour cream, thinly sliced avocado, and a sprinkle of chopped cilantro.

Dust with cayenne for added color *and* zing.

Substitute the pork with soy chorizo, making this meal vegetarian-"ish." I buy soy chorizo (sold in tubes) at my local dollar store of all places—*for just a buck!* These freeze well too, so I stock up and keep multiple logs in my freezer.

Splash your omelet with your favorite hot sauce to add flavor *but not carbs.*

BROWN BAG BLUEBERRY MUFFINS

✕ ◉ 🌿

My family doesn't go out to breakfast, even while on vacation. It's just too expensive! On quick trips, we pack a few of our morning favorites like Brown Bag Blueberry Muffins. I might surprise you with this one, but I bake these *without using an oven*. Instead, I cook them inside an Instant Pot®! Brown Bag Blueberry Muffins *à la Instant Pot®* compete with the chaffle as the most requested breakfast item from my family. *Warning:* Extremely delicious *and* addictive.

> 1½ cups superfine blanched almond flour
>
> 2 teaspoons baking powder
>
> ¼ teaspoon salt
>
> ½ cup 0g net carbs sweetener
>
> 3 tablespoons coconut flour
>
> ⅓ cup coconut oil, melted
>
> 1½ teaspoons pure vanilla extract
>
> 4 large eggs, beaten
>
> ⅔ cup fresh blueberries

1 In a large mixing bowl, combine all ingredients except blueberries to form a loose batter.

2 Gently fold in berries.

3 Ladle eight servings of batter evenly into a silicone muffin pan.

4 Add 1 cup water to bottom of Instant Pot®. Place muffin pan on top of trivet inside Instant Pot®.

5 Tent muffins using aluminum foil (helps prevent muffins from becoming too moist during cooking).

6 Close lid, close vent, and cook on high pressure for 25 minutes. Turn off Instant Pot® and release pressure.

7 Remove lid and let cool. Serve muffins warm or cold.

TOTAL COST	$9.42
COST PER SERVING	$1.17

NET CARBS

5G

SERVES 8

PER SERVING:

CALORIES	276
FAT	22G
PROTEIN	8G
SODIUM	231MG
FIBER	3G
CARBOHYDRATES	14G
NET CARBS	5G
SUGAR	3G
SUGAR ALCOHOL	6G

TIME

PREP TIME:	5 MINUTES
COOK TIME:	25 MINUTES

TIPS & OPTIONS

Shop wisely. Superfine almond flour often has fewer net carbs than regular almond flour.

If you don't have a fancy round insert to make muffins in the Instant Pot®, don't fret. I don't have one either! I made my own makeshift muffin tin by cutting apart an old silicone muffin mold. I stacked my muffin molds three deep using aluminum foil as a separator.

Resist the temptation to use frozen blueberries. When thawed, frozen berries become mushy and difficult to handle, turning the batter blue when mixing—blue food is *not appetizing*.

CHI-CHI'S BANKROLL BREAKFAST BURRITO

NET CARBS

2G

SERVES 1

PER SERVING:

CALORIES	408
FAT	35G
PROTEIN	17G
SODIUM	581MG
FIBER	0G
CARBOHYDRATES	2G
NET CARBS	2G
SUGAR	2G

TIME

PREP TIME:	10 MINUTES
COOK TIME:	15 MINUTES

TIPS & OPTIONS

Convert Chi-Chi's Bankroll Breakfast Burrito into a lunch or dinner burrito by substituting grilled chicken or beef for the breakfast sausage. Add raw lettuce, tomato, and onion. The egg "tortilla" works any time of day!

Season with hot sauce.

Other fun ingredients to use as burrito filling are sliced jalapeños, chopped olives, and/or chopped cilantro.

If your egg tortilla tears, don't fret. Turn your burrito into a country scramble instead. *No one will know unless you tell them!* Your secret is safe with me.

I'm a California transplant, which means I didn't grow up here. My exposure to Mexican food as a kid was limited to Midwestern Mexican fast food (Taco Bell) and infrequent trips to our neighborhood Chi-Chi's Mexican restaurant. My childhood version of a burrito was filled with fried ground beef and hunks of iceberg lettuce, and topped with cubes of Cracker Barrel sharp Cheddar cheese. *That's just embarrassing!* Thank goodness living in the West has taught me a few things like how to make a proper burrito (and the actual definition of *chi-chis*)!

1 tablespoon unsalted butter

2 large eggs

2 tablespoons heavy whipping cream

2 tablespoons crumbled breakfast sausage

½ tablespoon finely chopped green onion

½ tablespoon chopped fresh spinach

½ tablespoon chopped tomato

⅛ teaspoon salt

⅛ teaspoon black pepper

½ tablespoon shredded Cheddar cheese

1. In a small skillet over low heat, melt butter.

2. In a small bowl, whisk eggs and cream. Pour mixture into skillet, covering entire bottom. Cook 3–5 minutes until solid. Transfer egg "tortilla" to a serving plate.

3. In a medium nonstick skillet over medium heat, brown sausage, vegetables, salt, and pepper for 10 minutes, stirring regularly.

4. Pour cooked meat and vegetable mixture onto egg "tortilla," add cheese, and gently roll to form burrito.

5. Serve warm.

NICKEL AND DIME NUCLEAR EGG SAMMIE

✗

NET CARBS

2G

SERVES 1

PER SERVING:

CALORIES	384
FAT	30G
PROTEIN	19G
SODIUM	671MG
FIBER	2G
CARBOHYDRATES	4G
NET CARBS	2G
SUGAR	2G

TIME

| PREP TIME: | 2 MINUTES |
| COOK TIME: | 4½ MINUTES |

TIPS & OPTIONS »

Top with hot sauce for added flavor. One of my favorites is Crystal from the great state of Louisiana!

Substitute a patty of breakfast sausage for the bacon to build a more substantial meal.

Spicy mayo or pesto added to Nickel and Dime Nuclear Egg Sammie adds more flavor and fat, which as you know, keeps you feeling fuller for longer.

If you have more time or patience (*what's that?*), prepare the egg on the stovetop sunny-side up.

Make an extra one for later! These sandwiches travel well. Wrap in aluminum foil and take in the car.

Mornings can be stressful. I try to sleep in until the last possible second, which, admittedly, makes the morning routine hurried. Trying to get out the door fast, I often don't have time to "bust out a skillet." *Something has to give!* The Nickel and Dime Nuclear Egg Sammie is a fast solution for me on days like this when I don't have the change for the drive-thru. A hot and tasty breakfast that is "nuked" in the microwave? *Why, yes!* And did I mention it even has BREAD?

2 large eggs, divided
2 teaspoons coconut flour
1½ tablespoons full-fat mayonnaise, divided
⅛ teaspoon baking soda
1 tablespoon shredded Cheddar cheese
1 strip no-sugar-added bacon

1   In a small mixing bowl, whisk one egg with coconut flour, 1 tablespoon mayonnaise, and baking soda.

2   Evenly divide egg mixture into two small well-greased bowls. Cover and microwave separately for 60 seconds each.

3   Remove bowls from microwave.

4   Whisk second egg in a well-greased small bowl and microwave covered for 60–90 seconds; egg will rise.

5   Remove from microwave and add cheese.

6   Microwave bacon for 90 seconds on paper towel–lined plate with another paper towel on top. Remove and let cool. Cut in half.

7   Remove the two coconut flour and egg "buns" from bowls and put egg patty on one followed by bacon (both halves).

8   Spread remaining ½ tablespoon mayonnaise on other "bun." Top with second "bun" and you're now ready to eat. Stack the buns so the wide part is in the center of the sandwich. Since buns are formed in a small bowl, the base of the bun will be narrower than its top.

CHAPTER 5

SOUPS AND SALADS

When done right, homemade soups, stews, and chilis are so filling. They are easy to make and practical for people on a budget. Old vegetables look new again. A package of meat serves more than you might anticipate. When ingredients are thrown into a slow cooker, dinner is made without much effort at all! Soups are perfect for a lazy day or when payday is in the distant future.

I like how versatile the added fat can be in soup. Creamy soups don't have to be made with just half and half or HWC—cream cheese or sour cream are also forgiving substitutions. Broth soups become even more delicious with supplemented olive oil. In addition to adding flavor, the bold richness of added fat to soups keeps me feeling fuller for longer.

At restaurants, I often find myself ordering the "unlimited" soup and salad. It's not just the flavors I like; it's also the quantity of food I can eat! High-fat, low-sugar salad dressings make low-carb vegetables taste good enough to really enjoy, while the fiber in the vegetables slows me down and prevents overeating. Eating soups and salads always fills me up.

> It might sound crass, but sometimes my stomach has trouble notifying my brain that I've finally eaten enough.

I need all the help I can get! As a result, fiber has become my best friend.

CHECK CASHING CHOWDA

↻ ✕ ◉

| TOTAL COST | $9.76 |
| COST PER SERVING | $1.22 |

NET CARBS

3G

SERVES 8

PER SERVING:

CALORIES	275
FAT	24G
PROTEIN	8G
SODIUM	255MG
FIBER	1G
CARBOHYDRATES	4G
NET CARBS	3G
SUGAR	2G

TIME

| PREP TIME:* | 10 MINUTES |
| COOK TIME: | 27 MINUTES |

Every Friday as a kid, we would cash my dad's check on the way to Big Boy's to eat dinner. The complimentary soup and salad bar made this restaurant a big hit in my family. Memories of eating clam chowder, though, are clouded with reminders of how I stuffed packets of miniature oyster crackers in my pockets when no one was looking. Like with popcorn, I loved crunching on those little snacks! To this day, I fight the urge to covet oyster cracker packets from the salad bar.

1 medium ham bone, cooked and meat removed

6 cups water

½ pound no-sugar-added bacon, chopped

½ cup diced green onion

1 tablespoon minced garlic

1½ cups heavy whipping cream

¾ cup unsweetened almond milk

5 tablespoons full-fat cream cheese, softened

1 (10-ounce) can boiled baby clams, drained and chopped

2 cups finely chopped (½" or less) cauliflower

1 In a large stockpot, cover the ham bone with water and bring to boil. Reduce heat to medium-low and simmer covered for 3–4 hours stirring regularly.

2 In a separate large stockpot over medium heat, fry chopped bacon 5–7 minutes, stirring regularly. Transfer bacon to a medium bowl. Leave 2 tablespoons fat in pot and drain the rest.

3 Add green onion and garlic to the pot and fry 3–5 minutes.

4 To the pot with the onion and garlic, add 1 cup ham bone stock and remaining ingredients, except bacon, and stir to combine. Simmer 10–15 minutes, stirring regularly until cauliflower is soft. Remove from heat and let cool 10 minutes.

5 Cover and refrigerate remaining ham bone stock.

6 Serve warm in soup bowls topped with cooked bacon.

* *Does not include 3 hours to make stock.*

TIPS & OPTIONS

Serve Check Cashing Chowda with a sprinkle of fresh green onion, black pepper, or hot sauce.

Instead of pairing the soup with carby oyster crackers, try a few pork rinds instead.

Another salty option to accompany your soup is homemade cheese whisps. Reboot extra croutons made from the Capital Caesar Salad, Extra CROUTONS! recipe in this chapter.

Do you miss potatoes in clam chowder? Boil radishes—*yes radishes!*—and add a cup or so to this recipe. The trick is to really cook them well, like a ridiculously long amount of time.

NEST EGG DROP SOUP

As you build your pantry of DIRTY, LAZY, KETO ingredients, put xanthan gum high up on the list. You might be tempted to skip this unusual ingredient, but trust me, it really improves the consistency of Nest Egg Drop Soup. This emulsifier helps "bind" the soup's ingredients, thickening the broth similar to soups we are used to. Instead of using cornstarch or flour as additives, xanthan gum gets the job done without adding unnecessary carbs. One bag of xanthan gum will last you a lifetime.

6 cups water

5 (3.7-gram) cubes chicken-flavored bouillon

2 teaspoons minced garlic

2 teaspoons ground ginger

1 tablespoon soy sauce

1 teaspoon xanthan gum

3 large eggs, beaten

2 tablespoons finely chopped green onion

1 Pour water into a medium stockpot over medium heat, and stir in bouillon. Cover and bring to a boil. Reduce heat to simmer.

2 Add garlic, ginger, and soy sauce. Sprinkle xanthan gum in slowly while vigorously whisking to prevent potential clumping. Let covered pot simmer 10 minutes.

3 Slowly "drop" beaten eggs into soup using a thin pour (the simmering soup will flash cook the egg into ribbons).

4 Serve warm topped with green onion.

MANAGER'S SPECIAL STEAK SALAD

🍲 ✗ ◎

When you're on a tight budget, buying expensive meats isn't an option. I try to catch manager discounted steaks when they hit the clearance rack (this is a thing!), but if none are available, I do the next best thing: *marinate the meat.* By soaking a thinly cut inexpensive piece of meat overnight (the longer the better), steak becomes tender and more flavorful.

¼ pound flank steak, thinly sliced

2 tablespoons olive oil, divided

2 tablespoons steak seasoning

1 teaspoon minced garlic

1 tablespoon unsalted butter

½ large head iceberg lettuce, chopped

½ cup chopped green onion

1 cup chopped fresh spinach

1 cup chopped tomato

½ cup crumbled feta cheese

1   In a 2-gallon Ziploc bag, add steak, 1 tablespoon oil, seasoning, and garlic. Squeeze out as much air as you can before sealing. Knead meat through the bag to thoroughly coat with seasoning. Refrigerate overnight.

2   The next day, in a large saucepan over medium heat, melt butter. Add meat and cook 10–15 minutes while stirring until no longer red. Remove from heat.

3   Toss remaining ingredients in a large salad bowl. Drizzle with remaining olive oil.

4   Serve tossed salad greens on four plates and top each with ¼ of the cooked beef.

* Does not include 12 hours overnight marinate.

TOTAL COST	$7.60
COST PER SERVING	$1.90

NET CARBS

5G

SERVES 4

PER SERVING:	
CALORIES	169
FAT	11G
PROTEIN	11G
SODIUM	713MG
FIBER	2G
CARBOHYDRATES	7G
NET CARBS	5G
SUGAR	4G

TIME

PREP TIME:*	15 MINUTES
COOK TIME:	15 MINUTES

≪ TIPS & OPTIONS

Mix and match favorite low-carb vegetables or your preferred type of cheese in this recipe. Cucumbers, broccoli florets, or fresh mushrooms would make excellent choices.

If you prefer more of a dressing on your salad than just the olive oil, then go ahead and substitute a low-carb dressing. The sauce from Tiki Tiki Splurge Salad (see recipe in this chapter) is a great option.

Instead of buying steak seasoning, make your own house blend. Common ingredients include black pepper, paprika, onion powder, salt, dill, and red pepper.

ELOPIN' ON A SHOESTRING GUMBO

TOTAL COST $8.70
COST PER SERVING $1.45

NET CARBS

4G

SERVES 6

PER SERVING:

CALORIES	311
FAT	22G
PROTEIN	20G
SODIUM	1,372MG
FIBER	1G
CARBOHYDRATES	5G
NET CARBS	4G
SUGAR	1G

TIME

PREP TIME:	10 MINUTES
COOK TIME:	30 MINUTES

TIPS & OPTIONS

Serve on a bed of Payday Pork Fried "Rice" (see Chapter 8).

Slice sausage at a slight angle for a more authentic look.

Spice it up! Increase the Cajun fun by adding additional cayenne pepper.

Take your Creole experience to a whole new level by adding *gator* or *turtle* meat to your gumbo. I was surprised to discover alligator is sold both at local butchers and in superstores. I haven't tried it myself, but my brave husband and coauthor sure has! He described gator meat like super chewy dark meat chicken. Turtle meat on the other hand? The jury is still out.

One of my favorite NOLA (New Orleans) memories is when my husband and I rented bikes to explore the city. We were trying to find the plantation house where we eloped many moons ago. Since the location didn't pop up on any searches, we looked for the chapel using one unreliable clue: a picture from our wedding night where we sat in a horse-drawn carriage parked out front of a beautiful antebellum mansion. After a magical afternoon of bike riding, we finally found it (it had been converted back to a regular home)! To celebrate our discovery, we shared a jumbo bowl of Louisiana's finest gumbo—*sans rice, of course!*

1 tablespoon unsalted butter

½ cup chopped green onion

½ cup seeded and thinly sliced green bell pepper

2 medium stalks celery, sliced

½ pound (71–90 per pound size) shrimp, peeled, deveined, and tails off

1 pound precooked sausage, sliced

4 cups water

1 teaspoon Creole seasoning

1½ teaspoons paprika

1 In a large stockpot over medium heat, melt butter. Add onion, bell pepper, and celery and cook 5 minutes while stirring.

2 Stir in shrimp and sausage and brown 5 minutes while stirring.

3 Add remaining ingredients, bring to boil, then reduce heat, cover, and simmer 20 minutes, stirring regularly.

4 Let cool 10 minutes and serve warm.

TOTAL COST $6.38
COST PER SERVING $1.60

NET CARBS

5G

SERVES 4

PER SERVING:

CALORIES	412
FAT	33G
PROTEIN	16G
SODIUM	839MG
FIBER	3G
CARBOHYDRATES	8G
NET CARBS	5G
SUGAR	2G

TIME

PREP TIME:	10 MINUTES
COOK TIME:	7 MINUTES

TIPS & OPTIONS

Sardine phobic? Omit these fishy favorites.

Form the Cheddar cheese pinches as compact as possible (but not too flat) as they spread out when the cheese melts.

Instead of using Cheddar cheese to make croutons, try substituting finely shredded Parmesan cheese. This choice of cheese makes a more "adult" flavored whisp.

Crumble the hardened cheese chips into "croutons" as big or as small as you choose.

Double up the crouton portion of this recipe to reboot with Check Cashing Chowda or Treat Yo' Self Tomato Soup (see recipes in this chapter).

CAPITAL CAESAR SALAD, EXTRA CROUTONS!

One of the biggest challenges of eating healthy is knowing what to order in restaurants. It's tempting to revert back to "old favorites" when faced with a confusing array of choices. To help reduce decision anxiety, I recommend having a few standardized orders on the tip of your tongue. For me, some of my "go-to" menu choices include chicken wings, an omelet, or a chicken Caesar salad.

Croutons

1 cup shredded Cheddar cheese

⅛ teaspoon salt

Dressing

3 sardines, minced

½ cup full-fat mayonnaise

2 tablespoons grated Parmesan cheese

1 teaspoon minced garlic

1 teaspoon Worcestershire sauce

1 teaspoon yellow mustard

½ teaspoon 100% lemon juice from concentrate

⅛ teaspoon salt

⅛ teaspoon black pepper

Salad

1 large head romaine lettuce

½ cup grated Parmesan cheese

1 Preheat oven to 400°F. Line two baking sheets with parchment paper.

2 In a medium bowl, combine Cheddar cheese and salt. Place 1 teaspoon-sized pinches of salted cheese on baking sheets. Push flat and make sure they are not touching.

3 Bake 5–7 minutes until slightly brown. Let cool.

4 In a small bowl, add all dressing ingredients and mix well.

5 Chop lettuce and add to a large salad bowl. Toss with dressing.

6 Distribute salad mixture evenly into four salad bowls. Top with "croutons" and sprinkle with even amounts of Parmesan cheese.

7 Serve chilled.

BLUEBOOK BROCCOLI SALAD

My commitment to better health is strongest on Mondays. By Friday? Well…not so much! To capitalize on this predictable wax and wane pattern, I grocery shop and meal prep on Mondays. I often make Bluebook Broccoli Salad on Mondays and store the salad in a large Tupperware to eat throughout the week. Shortcuts like this help me to stay #dlkstrong even when I'm tired.

6 cups water

1 (12-ounce) bag fresh broccoli florets

1 cup full-fat mayonnaise

¼ cup full-fat sour cream

1 tablespoon 100% lemon juice

¼ cup 0g net carbs sweetener

¼ teaspoon salt

⅛ teaspoon black pepper

½ cup chopped red onion

¼ cup cooked and crumbled no-sugar-added bacon

¼ cup roasted sunflower seeds, hulled

1   In a large stockpot over medium heat, boil water. Add broccoli and boil 4–5 minutes to soften. Over sink, pour broccoli into metal colander and cool completely.

2   In a medium mixing bowl, whisk remaining ingredients until well blended and sweetener has dissolved. Fold in warm florets until completely coated in dressing.

3   Serve chilled in fancy salad bowls.

| TOTAL COST | $8.27 |
| COST PER SERVING | $1.03 |

NET CARBS

5G

SERVES 8

PER SERVING:

CALORIES	280
FAT	26G
PROTEIN	5G
SODIUM	372MG
FIBER	2G
CARBOHYDRATES	10G
NET CARBS	5G
SUGAR	2G
SUGAR ALCOHOL	3G

TIME

| PREP TIME: | 10 MINUTES |
| COOK TIME: | 5 MINUTES |

TIPS & OPTIONS

Prefer a crunchier salad? I often skip cooking the broccoli and make my broccoli salad using finely chopped raw florets.

Shorten prep time by microwaving the broccoli 2–3 minutes instead of the boiling method. Some broccoli packages are already washed and microwave ready (in the bag)! Talk about LAZY; *I'm lovin' it.*

Bluebook Broccoli Salad tastes better the next day when all the flavors have a chance to mix and meld.

As I enjoy leftovers of Bluebook Broccoli Salad, I top with a fresh sprinkle of crunchy bacon bits and sunflower seeds.

TIKI TIKI SPLURGE SALAD

I fell in love with Mediterranean food as a teenager. Not because of its purported health benefits, but because the waiter would yell *"Opa!"* when serving dishes of flaming cheese. Special occasions with my family have always been celebrated with food. Eating dinner in Greektown, located just outside of Detroit, was a special splurge in my family's limited budget. Greektown introduced me to my beloved tzatziki, or tiki tiki sauce.

Tiki Tiki Sauce

1 cup shredded cucumber

½ teaspoon salt

1 cup full-fat plain Greek yogurt

½ tablespoon white vinegar

1 tablespoon olive oil

1 teaspoon minced garlic

1 teaspoon dried dill weed

Salad

4 cups chopped romaine lettuce

1 cup halved grape tomatoes

1 cup sliced red onion

¼ cup sliced cucumber

½ cup pitted Kalamata olives

½ cup crumbled feta cheese

1   Place shredded cucumber in a colander with a plate underneath. Mix in salt with your hands and let mixture drain at least 4 hours. Stir every 30 minutes. Place a piece of parchment paper on cucumber shreds and push down every 30 minutes. Drain water from the plate as it accumulates.

2   After cucumber shreds have drained, place them in a medium bowl and stir in remaining sauce ingredients. Cover and refrigerate.

3   In a large salad bowl, add all the salad ingredients and toss to combine.

4   Serve salad with ¼ cup chilled tiki tiki sauce per serving.

* Includes 4 hours drain time.

TOTAL COST	$9.85
COST PER SERVING	$2.46

NET CARBS

8G

SERVES 4

PER SERVING:

CALORIES	202
FAT	15G
PROTEIN	9G
SODIUM	738MG
FIBER	2G
CARBOHYDRATES	10G
NET CARBS	8G
SUGAR	6G

TIME

PREP TIME:*	4 HOURS 15 MINUTES
COOK TIME:	0 MINUTES

TIPS & OPTIONS

You might have some leftover tiki tiki sauce for later. I like to dip raw vegetables in tiki tiki for an afternoon snack. Another idea is to reboot the dressing on top of Manager's Special Steak Salad (see recipe in this chapter).

Make your meal more robust by topping the salad with grilled lamb or shrimp. Flavor your meat with Cavender's All Purpose Greek Seasoning, which is 0 grams of net carbs per a serving size of ¼ teaspoon.

Reboot the Reduced Rate Rosemary Kabobs (see Chapter 9) by using that leftover meat served on top of this salad.

COST CONSCIOUS CAVEMAN SOUP

NET CARBS

0G

SERVES 4

PER SERVING:

CALORIES	16
FAT	1G
PROTEIN	2G
SODIUM	7MG
FIBER	0G
CARBOHYDRATES	0G
NET CARBS	0G
SUGAR	0G

TIME

PREP TIME:	2 MINUTES
COOK TIME:	90 MINUTES

TIPS & OPTIONS

Get in the habit of saving your chicken and turkey carcasses after finishing a whole bird at home. Seal and freeze for later use.

If you are feeling fancy, add minced garlic, diced onion, celery, and carrots to the pot before boiling. Wilted vegetables? *You betcha!* They only add flavor, not appearance.

I prefer not to add salt or pepper since this stock will be used in other recipes with their own seasonings.

Reboot leftover Cost Conscious Caveman Soup to other recipes in this chapter, such as Rainy Day Soup, Chump Change Chili, Treat Yo' Self Tomato Soup, or Nest Egg Drop Soup.

The process of ketosis (fat-burning mode) requires a lot of fluids. It's easy to become dehydrated if you aren't careful! To avoid the uncomfortable side effects of the much-feared **keto flu** (headache, leg cramps, tiredness) be sure to drink electrolyte-rich fluids. I recommend drinking sugar-free sports drinks, pickle juice, or homemade broth such as Cost Conscious Caveman Soup to keep yourself in balance. It only requires bones and water heated over fire. I consider Cost Conscious Caveman Soup a zero-cost food item since the carcass was a "throwaway" item from a previous meal.

1 whole chicken carcass from medium cooked chicken, stripped of meat

4 cups water

1 In a large stockpot over medium heat, submerge the carcass in water.

2 Cover and bring to boil, then reduce heat to low.

3 Simmer 90 minutes while covered, stirring every 20 minutes.

4 Remove from heat and let cool.

5 When cool enough to handle, strain stock using a cheesecloth or fine colander. Discard filtered bone/skin matter.

6 Pour into a large food storage container and refrigerate until needed.

CHUMP CHANGE CHILI

Living in California, I've learned a handful of useful Spanish words. Mainly, these have to do with food (since I love to eat!). The Spanish word *chili* actually comes from the phrase *chili con carne*, which translates to "meat with chiles." You see, even the Spanish didn't add beans! Just like the conquistadors before us, Chump Change Chili is rich with tradition. It keeps familiar chili flavors while abandoning unnecessary carbs.

- 1½ pounds boneless, skinless chicken breasts
- 2 medium jalapeños, deveined, seeded, and minced
- ¾ cup seeded and finely chopped green bell pepper
- ½ cup chopped yellow onion
- 1 (4-ounce) can diced green chiles
- 1 tablespoon minced garlic
- 1½ tablespoons ground cumin
- 3½ cups chicken stock
- ¼ teaspoon salt
- ¼ teaspoon black pepper
- 1½ (8-ounce) packages full-fat cream cheese, softened

1 To a large stockpot over medium heat, add all ingredients except cream cheese.

2 Cover and bring to boil and then reduce heat to simmer for 1 hour, stirring occasionally.

3 Remove from heat and finely shred chicken with fork.

4 Add cream cheese and return to low/medium heat while covered for 15 minutes, stirring regularly.

5 Remove from heat; let cool at least 15 minutes and serve.

TOTAL COST	$9.36
COST PER SERVING	$1.17

NET CARBS

8G

SERVES 8

PER SERVING:

CALORIES	302
FAT	15G
PROTEIN	25G
SODIUM	466MG
FIBER	1G
CARBOHYDRATES	9G
NET CARBS	8G
SUGAR	4G

TIME

PREP TIME:	20 MINUTES
COOK TIME:	75 MINUTES

TIPS & OPTIONS

Suggested toppings are a dash of hot sauce, a spoonful of sour cream, avocado slices, fresh onion bits, and/or chopped cilantro.

Have you tried black soybeans? They look and taste just like traditional black beans but only have 3.5 grams of net carbs per 15-ounce can. Add black soybeans to the recipe for a more traditional chili look and taste. Because I haven't been able to find them in stores, I buy canned black soybeans in bulk online.

Here's another reboot opportunity to utilize leftover stock from Cost Conscious Caveman Soup (see recipe in this chapter).

TYCOON TITANIC WEDGE SALAD

TOTAL COST $6.27
COST PER SERVING $1.57

NET CARBS

5G

SERVES 4

PER SERVING:
CALORIES	331
FAT	24G
PROTEIN	18G
SODIUM	943MG
FIBER	3G
CARBOHYDRATES	8G
NET CARBS	5G
SUGAR	5G

TIME

PREP TIME:	10 MINUTES
COOK TIME:	0 MINUTES

TIPS & OPTIONS

I recommend quartering the un-cored head of lettuce at the stem so the four wedges are easier to handle. For each wedge, the lettuce leaves will be attached at the corner where the core is.

Buy blue cheese salad dressing at the store instead of making it from scratch.

Remember Bac-Os from the 1970s? They taste terrific sprinkled on Tycoon Titanic Wedge Salad. They are made from soy, so technically, will fall into the vegetarian-"ish" category.

Boost your protein by serving with a side of grilled shrimp or chicken, or slices of hard-boiled eggs.

Did iceberg lettuce hire a publicist? This inexpensive lettuce is dressed to impress in the Tycoon Titanic Wedge Salad. With all the delicious distractions piled on top, you won't notice the plain (and inexpensive!) iceberg greens underneath. Be dramatic when serving your wedge. Just like the *Titanic*, build it "the bigger the better"!

Salad
1 large head iceberg lettuce
½ cup diced tomato
1 (4-ounce) package blue cheese crumbles, divided
¼ pound no-sugar-added bacon, cooked and crumbled

Blue Cheese Dressing
2 tablespoons full-fat mayonnaise
2 tablespoons full-fat sour cream
2 tablespoons half and half
½ tablespoon white vinegar
⅛ teaspoon salt
⅛ teaspoon black pepper

1 Quarter the head of lettuce. Set each quarter on its own salad plate.

2 Top each evenly with tomatoes, 2 ounces cheese crumbles, and bacon.

3 Make the dressing: In a medium bowl, whisk all dressing ingredients together with remaining 2 ounces cheese crumbles.

4 Evenly top each wedge with dressing. Serve chilled.

RAINY DAY SOUP

Newbies to the low-carb/high-fat lifestyle often complain about contracting the keto flu and therefore think about quitting. Let me tell it to you straight: The keto flu *is not* a real sickness! Kind of like a hangover, it's actually dehydration and an electrolyte imbalance that causes these symptoms: headaches, tiredness, and leg cramps. By proactively increasing liquids and electrolytes, the keto flu can be entirely avoided. Rainy Day Soup is packed with valuable, high-electrolyte foods like spinach, cashew milk, tofu, chicken stock, and salt.

1 (16-ounce) package extra firm tofu, drained, cut into ¼" cubes

3 tablespoons unsalted butter

½ cup chopped green onion

1 cup sliced mushrooms

3 cups unsweetened plain cashew milk

3 cups chicken stock

2 teaspoons salt

½ teaspoon black pepper

1 teaspoon minced garlic

4 cups chopped fresh spinach

1½ cups shredded Cheddar cheese

1 In a medium nonstick skillet over medium heat, brown tofu cubes 10–13 minutes, stirring regularly to brown all sides.

2 Melt butter in a large stockpot over medium heat, then add onion and mushrooms. Brown onion and mushrooms 10–12 minutes while stirring.

3 Add tofu and remaining ingredients except cheese and bring to boil. Cover and reduce heat to simmer. Cook 20 minutes, stirring regularly.

4 Remove from heat and let cool 15 minutes. Blend soup with immersion hand blender on high 2–5 minutes to remove spinach clumps.

5 Bring pot back to boil over medium heat and stir in cheese until completely melted for approximately 10 minutes.

6 Remove from heat and let cool 15 minutes. Serve.

CHANGE PURSE CUCUMBER SALAD

Ordering low-carb food is so easy at a Japanese hibachi-style restaurant. You know the type of place…parties of ten seated around knife-wielding chefs who build fire-breathing volcanos out of onions and oil. Hibachi food is a credit to the DLK lifestyle: high in fat, moderate in protein, and low in carbs. *I feel at home!* Change Purse Cucumber Salad recipe reminds me of the first course served at Japanese hibachi restaurants.

> 3 medium cucumbers, thinly sliced
>
> ¼ teaspoon salt
>
> ½ cup apple cider vinegar
>
> 2 tablespoons olive oil
>
> ¼ teaspoon crushed red pepper flakes
>
> ¼ teaspoon sriracha sauce
>
> 3 tablespoons 0g net carbs sweetener
>
> ⅓ cup chopped red onion
>
> 1 cup halved grape tomatoes

1 In a large salad bowl, toss all ingredients together.
2 Chill until ready to serve.

TOTAL COST	$6.06
COST PER SERVING	$1.01

NET CARBS

4G

SERVES 6

PER SERVING:

CALORIES	71
FAT	5G
PROTEIN	1G
SODIUM	106MG
FIBER	1G
CARBOHYDRATES	11G
NET CARBS	4G
SUGAR	4G
SUGAR ALCOHOL	6G

TIME

PREP TIME:	10 MINUTES
COOK TIME:	0 MINUTES

TIPS & OPTIONS

Try substituting chopped beefsteak or Roma tomatoes for the grape tomatoes.

Stir Change Purse Cucumber Salad regularly as cucumbers will release water into the dressing.

In the mood for Greek instead of spicy? Substitute sriracha sauce with 1 teaspoon Greek-blend seasoning and top salad with crumbled feta cheese.

Round out the salad into a full meal by adding grilled shrimp or chicken on the side.

TREAT YO' SELF TOMATO SOUP

Artist Andy Warhol showcased pop-culture icons like the Campbell's Soup can in his screen printing. There is real beauty in that kind of simplicity. This philosophy applies to DIRTY, LAZY, KETO—when in doubt, go back to the basics. Losing weight doesn't have to be complicated! Meals don't have to be elaborate to be delicious. Treat yourself to a simple cup of tomato soup tonight.

2 tablespoons unsalted butter

2 teaspoons minced garlic

1 (24-ounce) can no-sugar-added pasta sauce

2 cups vegetable broth

¾ cup full-fat cream cheese, softened

1 tablespoon 0g net carbs sweetener

⅛ teaspoon salt

⅛ teaspoon black pepper

½ teaspoon dried basil

1 In a large stockpot over medium heat, melt butter. Add garlic and brown 2–3 minutes while stirring.

2 Add remaining ingredients (except basil) to pot and bring to boil while stirring. Cover, reduce heat to medium-high, and simmer 20 minutes. Remove from heat.

3 Serve with sprinkle of basil on top.

TOTAL COST	$4.09
COST PER SERVING	$0.68

NET CARBS

6G

SERVES 6

PER SERVING:

CALORIES	169
FAT	13G
PROTEIN	3G
SODIUM	965MG
FIBER	3G
CARBOHYDRATES	9G
NET CARBS	6G
SUGAR	5G

TIME

PREP TIME:	10 MINUTES
COOK TIME:	23 MINUTES

TIPS & OPTIONS

Make extra and freeze for another meal.

Instead of a grilled cheese sandwich (which arguably pairs PERFECTLY with a cup of tomato soup), reboot the cheese croutons made in the Capital Caesar Salad, Extra CROUTONS! recipe in this chapter to enjoy crumbled on top.

Consider using rebooted leftover chicken stock here from your Cost Conscious Caveman Soup (see recipe in this chapter).

Commercially packaged pasta sauce is usually loaded with added sugar. Read those nutrition labels carefully! Two popular brands I rely on are Hunt's (no-sugar-added) and Rao's Homemade.

SCRATCH THE EGG FAST SALAD SANDWICH

TIPS & OPTIONS »

Lettuce, tomato, and onion are all suitable additions.

Serve sandwich with a side of dill pickle. Save the pickle juice for later! Pickle juice is a natural and inexpensive electrolyte fluid.

Crispy bacon bits give this egg salad a little snap. Doesn't everything taste better with bacon?

Try adding a spoonful of store-bought pesto or dollop of Start a Tab Tapas Spread (see Chapter 8) to your egg salad mixture.

Make double the "buns" hon, and you'll have enough for the Stockpile Sliders (see Chapter 9), rebooted tomorrow!

In my observation, folks voluntarily enter an all-out egg eating binge for one of three reasons: *desperation, guilt, or punishment.* No matter what your motivation, I'm here to encourage a happier relationship with eggs.

Buns

2 ounces full-fat cream cheese, softened

6 ounces shredded whole milk mozzarella cheese

1 large egg, beaten

1 clove garlic, minced

⅓ cup superfine blanched almond flour

½ tablespoon baking powder

4 ounces shredded Cheddar cheese

Egg Salad Filling

4 large eggs, hard-boiled

⅓ cup full-fat mayonnaise

½ teaspoon prepared yellow mustard

¼ cup finely chopped green onion

⅛ teaspoon salt

⅛ teaspoon black pepper

⅛ teaspoon paprika

1 In a medium microwave-safe bowl, add cream cheese and mozzarella cheese. Microwave 30 seconds, stir, and microwave again for 30 seconds until fully melted.

2 In another medium bowl, whisk egg, garlic, almond flour, and baking powder.

3 Fold egg mixture into cheese mixture. Fold in Cheddar cheese.

4 Form mixture into a ball and put in fridge 30 minutes.

5 Preheat oven to 425°F. Cover a baking sheet with greased foil.

6 Remove dough from fridge and divide it into four even balls. Distribute balls on baking sheet 2" apart.

7 Bake 10–15 minutes until browned.

8 Let cool 10 minutes. Slice horizontally to create two "bun" halves from each roll. Set aside.

9 Peel hard-boiled eggs. In a medium bowl, mash eggs with a fork.

10 Stir in remaining ingredients until thoroughly combined. Evenly distribute egg mixture onto the buns. Serve.

* Includes 30 minutes of setup time in the fridge.

CHAPTER 6

SNACKS

I get nervous when someone tells me I can't eat. Don't laugh, but at any given moment I probably have a snack (*or two, or three*) in my purse. If I'm walking to the mailbox or heading out to do errands, my immediate impulse is to pack food and water with me. Being hungry isn't the issue here. I just feel safer having snacks with me. *Is that so wrong?*

We eat for many reasons other than hunger. I believe emotional triggers to eat are just as valid as physical desires. Here's the part that might surprise you, though. *I don't think my emotional eating needs "fixing."* As a middle-aged woman, my habits aren't likely to change. I've always reached for food when I'm nervous, stressed, excited, or anxious. Having a snack just calms me down.

Instead of "beating myself up," I've found much more success in working *with* my habits. I don't judge myself or feel embarrassed about my love of snacks. I've completely let go of the "you shouldn't snack between meals" mentality and embraced who I really am: a frequent eater. That's not going to change. *I love to eat!*

I've learned to choose healthier foods for my snacks. I'm well aware that all this mindless eating "adds up," so I deliberately graze on low net carb foods that aren't likely to cause weight gain. You are likely to find a gallon-sized Ziploc bag of celery stalks in my car at this very moment!

If you're a snacker like me, let go of the shame. You are perfect just the way you are!

NET CARBS

7G

SERVES 6

PER SERVING:

CALORIES	251
FAT	18G
PROTEIN	12G
SODIUM	1,173MG
FIBER	5G
CARBOHYDRATES	12G
NET CARBS	7G
SUGAR	3G

TIME

PREP TIME: 15 MINUTES
COOK TIME: 0 MINUTES

TIPS & OPTIONS ≫

Substitute the feta cheese for Cheddar cubes. Really, any firm cheese will do.

When slicing and chopping the vegetables, keep in mind that they will be put on a skewer. Don't cut the pieces too small.

Fresh basil leaves and marinated mushrooms add a surprising twist to these kabobs.

Instead of using salami on your kabobs, get creative. Include folded pieces of leftover deli lunch meat instead.

Make sure that your feta cheese cubes are large enough to run a skewer through, ½"–1".

DEBT DIET POLICE KABOBS

✕ ◎

When I first started DIRTY, LAZY, KETO, I was afraid to eat anywhere except my house. I didn't want to explain my "new life-style" to anyone; I feared the diet police! Well-meaning (or rude) friends and relatives tend to give you an earful of unwanted advice once they hear you've started a "diet." I have many DLK "clones" that I whip out in these instances. One such incognito dish is the Debt Diet Police Kabobs—this antipasto dish won't give away your DLK secret, but if you get discovered…at least you'll be armed with a weapon.

½ cup pitted black olives

½ cup pitted green olives

1 (7-ounce) package sliced salami

1 cup fresh whole spinach leaves

1 (14-ounce) can artichoke hearts, drained, cut no bigger than ¾"

½ cup feta cheese cubes

1 cup seeded and chopped orange bell pepper

1 cup sliced cucumber

1 cup sliced yellow squash

1 cup whole cherry tomatoes

1 tablespoon olive oil

1   Thread ingredients on six long wooden skewers, using same order for all, with one cherry tomato at tip.

2   Artfully arrange Debt Diet Police Kabobs on platter and drizzle with olive oil.

RENT MONEY 'RONI CHIPS

TOTAL COST	$2.64
COST PER SERVING	$0.44

NET CARBS

0G

SERVES 6

PER SERVING:

CALORIES	186
FAT	13G
PROTEIN	9G
SODIUM	665MG
FIBER	0G
CARBOHYDRATES	0G
NET CARBS	0G
SUGAR	0G

TIME

PREP TIME:	1 MINUTE
COOK TIME:	8 MINUTES

TIPS & OPTIONS

Dip your Rent Money 'Roni Chips into leftover tiki tiki sauce, rebooting it from the Tiki Tiki Splurge Salad (see Chapter 5).

How about turkey pepperoni? This substitute ingredient works just as well!

Bake your chips with a small pinch of cheese on them topped with some diced olives or jalapeños.

Enjoy this snack instead of popcorn at the movie theater.

Double (or quadruple) the recipe so you have enough to bring on your next weekend barbecue with friends or the next Big Game Party.

There is something about watching mindless television that requires one to crave chips. Salty, easy to grab, CHIPS! While potatoes are in my rearview mirror, I am always trying to discover a "next best" alternative. As I shared in *The DIRTY, LAZY, KETO® Cookbook: Bend the Rules to Lose the Weight!*, one of my favorite sitcom-watching pastimes is to eat artichoke chips. If those aren't in season (or I'm feeling too lazy to cook one!), Rent Money 'Roni Chips are next on the hit list. Serve with your choice of dip.

½ pound pepperoni slices

1 Preheat oven to 400°F. Line a baking sheet with parchment paper.

2 Evenly spread pepperoni on sheet with no overlapping.

3 Bake 5–8 minutes until brown and crisp.

4 Let cool slightly and serve.

ROCK BOTTOM SCRIMP COCKTAIL

✗ ◉

When I go to parties, I always bring a "safe" DLK dish. I have a short list of favorites to draw upon, and bringing Rock Bottom Scrimp Cocktail ranks high on the list. *It's so fancy!* I want to enjoy the party, not stress about what food is being served.

¾ cup no-sugar-added ketchup

¾ cup mild salsa

1½ teaspoons 100% lemon juice

1½ tablespoons horseradish

⅛ teaspoon hot sauce

½ pound (51–60 per pound size) shrimp, cooked

1 Add all ingredients except shrimp to food processor and pulse 15–30 seconds until blended and desired consistency.

2 Add to a medium-sized decorative bowl.

3 Place bowl on a large plate and spread shrimp around bowl (on plate).

4 Serve chilled.

| TOTAL COST | $7.05 |
| COST PER SERVING | $0.59 |

NET CARBS

2G

SERVES 12

PER SERVING:

CALORIES	33
FAT	0G
PROTEIN	4G
SODIUM	485MG
FIBER	1G
CARBOHYDRATES	3G
NET CARBS	2G
SUGAR	2G

TIME

| PREP TIME: | 5 MINUTES |
| COOK TIME: | 0 MINUTES |

≪ TIPS & OPTIONS

Buy frozen shrimp in bulk to keep costs down. Freeze remaining shrimp for your next special event. Don't laugh, but I have a chest freezer in my garage full of goodies like this! I'm like a DLK Girl Scout—always prepared. I'm ready to be invited to any party!

I prefer to buy pre-cleaned shrimp. I don't want to spend my afternoon peeling shells and deveining shrimp. That's one activity I don't enjoy!

Add more or less hot sauce according to your taste.

Serve platter on a bed of ice—*safety first!*

WEEKLY ALLOWANCE ARTICHOKE DIP

TOTAL COST $6.47
COST PER SERVING $0.54

NET CARBS

4G

SERVES 12

My mantra for DLK is to make healthy food taste better. Adding fat (a.k.a. goop) to vegetables makes them tolerable (if not enjoyable!). That being said, I've been known to get a little carried away when it comes to dipping raw veggies in goop. It's easy for me to go overboard with eating dips. I like quantity! As the self-appointed hall monitor for my dipping, I've instituted an "every other" dipping strategy. Eating one stalk of naked veggie allows me a dip with goop in the next go-around.

PER SERVING:

CALORIES	185
FAT	17G
PROTEIN	2G
SODIUM	338MG
FIBER	1G
CARBOHYDRATES	5G
NET CARBS	4G
SUGAR	1G

1 (14-ounce) can artichoke hearts

½ (8-ounce) package full-fat cream cheese, softened

1 cup full-fat mayonnaise

¼ cup grated Parmesan cheese

½ (1-ounce) package ranch dressing mix

1 large zucchini, sliced into ⅛"–¼"–thick rounds

TIME

PREP TIME:	10 MINUTES
COOK TIME:	20 MINUTES

1 Preheat oven to 375°F. Grease a 9" × 9" × 2" baking dish.

2 Drain water from artichoke hearts and finely chop.

3 Add artichokes and remaining ingredients, except zucchini, to a medium mixing bowl and mix well.

4 Scrape mixture into a baking dish and cover with foil.

5 Bake 20 minutes until bubbly, removing foil for last 7–10 minutes to brown.

6 Serve warm with zucchini medallions to scoop dip.

TIPS & OPTIONS

More (or less) vegetables can be finely chopped and served in this dip. I try to eat as many vegetables a day as possible. On Mondays, when my willpower is strongest, I wash and prep raw vegetables for the week.

Sliced cucumbers, zucchini spears, bell pepper slices, broccoli florets, and cauliflower florets can all be used to scoop the dip.

The trick with dips is portion control. Instead of sitting down with the full Pyrex dish of warm dip (which we've all done!), scoop out a meaningful portion and walk away from the mothership.

"BALLER ON A BUDGET" BEER BOILED NUTS

✗ ✿

I could eat nuts by the bucketful! I love their salty deliciousness. Since my tendency is to overeat nuts (of any kind!), I have to work hard at maintaining a sense of portion control. I don't give myself free rein with a container of nuts; that would be disastrous! Instead, I use a shot glass to scoop out a handful.

2 pounds green peanuts, in the shell

1 tablespoon minced garlic

½ cup salt

¼ cup chopped green onion

2½ cups water

1 (12-ounce) can beer, any style

1 Add all ingredients to a large stockpot and bring to boil. Cover, reduce heat to medium, and let simmer 1½–2 hours until tender and salty.

2 Remove from heat and let peanuts soak at least 2 hours but preferably overnight.

3 Drain the water and serve in small bowls while still in shell.

* Includes 2 hours soak time.

TIPS & OPTIONS

Any beer will do. (It doesn't have to be a low-carb type.) Only a negligible amount of beer will remain on the nuts and be consumed.

Freshly picked raw peanuts are "green peanuts." "Raw peanuts" are usually dried; they require a longer cook time.

Keep peanuts in the shells/ pods until they are finally eaten.

Boiled nuts in the shell are best enjoyed outside where opening the shell doesn't leave behind a huge mess. Enjoy "Baller on a Budget" Beer Boiled Nuts at a barbecue or on a hike. This snack travels well.

SLIDING SCALE SUSHI SHOT

TOTAL COST $0.54
COST PER SERVING $0.27

NET CARBS

1G

SERVES 2

This might sound weird, but eating Sliding Scale Sushi Shots makes me think I'm eating a California Roll. It must be the combination of avocado and soy sauce that fools my brain! Yes, I'm sure that I could probably find a fancy-pants sushi restaurant to make me a custom, low-carb roll using cucumber and avocado slices, but this recipe is much cheaper (and faster). Try it and tell me what you think. I'll be sure and thank my mother-in-law—who admittedly came up with this strange idea when trying to figure out how to eat a rapidly ripening bag of avocados—for you.

PER SERVING:

CALORIES	114
FAT	9G
PROTEIN	2G
SODIUM	150MG
FIBER	5G
CARBOHYDRATES	6G
NET CARBS	1G
SUGAR	0G

TIME

PREP TIME:	1 MINUTE
COOK TIME:	0 MINUTES

1 medium ripe avocado

1 teaspoon soy sauce, divided

1   Slice avocado in half lengthwise and remove pit.

2   Leaving skin on, hold one of the avocado halves with rounded side down and add ½ teaspoon soy sauce into semicircular space that pit used to occupy. Repeat with the other half.

3   Slowly scoop out avocado flesh with a spoon, being sure to get some soy sauce in each spoonful.

« TIPS & OPTIONS

Top with a pinch of garlic powder for more depth of flavor.

I'm lucky to live in California where avocados can be grown at home or bought year-round at roadside stands. I buy our avocados by the bag, usually for no more than $2–$3, so Sliding Scale Sushi Shots come in handy when the avocados ripen at the same time. Freeze peeled avocado chunks for later use. *Really!*

My husband likes to eat these while standing over the kitchen sink. The soy sauce always seems to spill a little, so this technique saves valuable cleanup time. *Lazy Keto, remember?*

BOGO BACON JALAPEÑO DOG

⊙

TOTAL COST	$6.10
COST PER SERVING	$0.76

NET CARBS

2G

SERVES 8

PER SERVING:

CALORIES	169
FAT	12G
PROTEIN	12G
SODIUM	522MG
FIBER	0G
CARBOHYDRATES	2G
NET CARBS	2G
SUGAR	1G

TIME

PREP TIME:	5 MINUTES
COOK TIME:	25 MINUTES

TIPS & OPTIONS ≫

Don food-grade gloves when prepping jalapeños to prevent the dreaded "jalapeño fingers." Otherwise, you risk transferring "burning" jalapeño oil from your fingers to anything you touch (like your eyes).

I like Aidells brand sausages. They come precooked, which saves me time in the kitchen. *Just heat and serve!* Plus, they come in all sorts of fun flavors like Cajun-style andouille or artichoke and garlic.

Don't worry if your sausage and jalapeño aren't exactly the same length. The unexpected assembly is part of the fun!

Hot dog buns are for wimps. Wrap your hot dog or sausage inside a jalapeño instead! These surprising bun alternatives will be the hit of any adult *par-tay*. It's this kind of outside-the-box thinking that makes DLK so much fun! BOGO Bacon Jalapeño Dogs are best enjoyed while drinking low-carb beer and watching the game.

8 jumbo-sized jalapeños

1 (12-ounce) package smoked chicken sausage, cooked

4 (1-ounce) slices Cheddar cheese, halved

4 slices cooked no-sugar-added bacon, cut in half

1 Prep jalapeños by cutting them in half lengthwise and carefully removing all veins and seeds.

2 In a covered medium stockpot, steam jalapeños in 1"-deep boiling water, 10–15 minutes until softened. Let cool enough to handle. Pat dry.

3 Slice sausages lengthwise, creating eight long, thin sausages.

4 Fill a medium skillet with ½" water and bring to boil.

5 Reduce heat to medium-high, add the sausages, and simmer 8–10 minutes, flipping halfway through.

6 Use two jalapeño halves as "buns." Wrap a still-hot sausage in a cheese slice and place in one pepper half. Place a half slice bacon on top of cheese-wrapped sausage and top with matching pepper half.

7 Repeat until all eight BOGO Bacon Jalapeño Dogs are complete. Serve warm.

BOURBON BORROWED SMOKIES

✗ ◉

I've never been one to sit still and watch "the game." I'd rather be in the kitchen making *or eating* snacks if I'm being completely honest! My husband thinks my Bourbon Borrowed Smokies recipe finished off his bottle of whiskey, but you'll soon find out the real truth. There might be a little "somethin' somethin'" here just for you.

> 2 (14-ounce) packages beef cocktail franks
>
> ½ cup 0g net carbs brown sugar alternative
>
> 1⅓ cups sugar-free barbecue sauce
>
> ½ tablespoon Worcestershire sauce
>
> 2 (1½-ounce) shots unflavored bourbon (one for the recipe and one for you!)

1. Add all ingredients to a slow cooker. Stir to mix.
2. Cook covered on low temperature for 2 hours.
3. Pour into a large decorative bowl and serve.

TRUST FUND TRAIL MIX

✕ ◉ ✿

Going to the movies and NOT ordering popcorn has been the biggest struggle in my weight loss journey. I try to tell myself that I'm saving loads of money by avoiding the concession stand, but the smell of carbolicious, buttery popcorn tempts me back to the dark side. Don't laugh, but the only way I'm able to go to the movies is by filling my purse with unauthorized DIRTY, LAZY, KETO contraband snacks like Trust Fund Trail Mix. It's salty and sweet!

¼ cup coconut oil, melted

½ cup 0g net carbs sweetener

1 teaspoon salt

2 teaspoons ground cinnamon

½ cup pecan halves

¼ cup shelled (same as hulled) hemp hearts

¼ cup shelled pumpkin seeds

¼ cup walnut halves

¼ cup whole almonds

¼ cup shredded unsweetened coconut

1 Preheat oven to 350°F. Line a baking sheet with parchment paper.

2 In a large bowl, combine oil, sweetener, salt, and cinnamon until sweetener and salt dissolve. Fold in the remaining ingredients until nuts are coated.

3 Spread evenly on baking sheet. Bake 15 minutes while stirring to prevent sticking. Remove from heat when starting to darken.

4 Let cool, then serve.

TOTAL COST	$7.85
COST PER SERVING	$0.79

NET CARBS

1G

SERVES 10

PER SERVING:

CALORIES	173
FAT	16G
PROTEIN	4G
SODIUM	232MG
FIBER	2G
CARBOHYDRATES	3G
NET CARBS	1G
SUGAR	1G

TIME

PREP TIME:	5 MINUTES
COOK TIME:	15 MINUTES

« TIPS & OPTIONS

Substitute any type of low-carb nut. Macadamia or Brazil nuts are terrific choices.

Want another movie theater snack idea? I bring a gallon-sized bag of cut-up celery with a portion-controlled travel-sized cup of peanut butter for dipping. Be sure to grab some salt packets as you power walk by the concession stand!

When I'm feeling extra frisky, sometimes I add Lily's sugar-free chocolate chips or Atkins Endulge Chocolate Candies to my serving of Trust Fund Trail Mix. It's *heavenly* but extremely addictive. Enjoy decadent treats like this with caution.

SPECIAL OFFER CERVEZA DIP

✕ ◉ ✿

I laughed out loud when I marked the Special Offer Cerveza Dip recipe as fancy enough for guests. I should have placed an asterisk and specified, *"well at my house, anyway!"* I don't consider myself a formal person. When we entertain guests, we are usually wearing wet swimming suits and flip-flops. Special Offer Cerveza Dip is worthy of sharing with your friends because it's fun (made with beer? *Hello!*) and tastes fabulous. No one will suspect you are trying to lose weight!

1½ cups shredded Cheddar cheese

1½ (8-ounce) packages full-fat cream cheese, softened

1 (1-ounce) packet ranch dressing mix

¾ cup low-carb beer

1   In a large, decorative, microwave-safe bowl, combine Cheddar cheese, cream cheese, and ranch dressing mix. Cover and microwave 1 minute (it will pop a little bit and make a mess of your microwave if not covered). Stir, cover again, and microwave 30 seconds.

2   Slowly stir in beer, cover, and microwave 60 seconds. Stir, cover again, and microwave for a final 30 seconds.

3   Stir and serve. Enjoy immediately to prevent the dreaded stiff dip.

| TOTAL COST | $4.74 |
| COST PER SERVING | $0.48 |

NET CARBS

3G

SERVES 10

PER SERVING:

CALORIES	197
FAT	15G
PROTEIN	6G
SODIUM	446MG
FIBER	0G
CARBOHYDRATES	3G
NET CARBS	3G
SUGAR	1G

TIME

| PREP TIME: | 5 MINUTES |
| COOK TIME: | 3 MINUTES |

TIPS & OPTIONS

Low net carb beer examples are Michelob ULTRA and Corona Premier. Note that this recipe only calls for ¾ cup of beer—*the rest of the six-pack is yours to share!*

Spice up your dip by adding a can of Rotel or finely chopped jalapeño. As always, remember to carefully seed and devein fresh jalapeños.

Serve with hearty raw vegetables like zucchini circles or spears, raw cauliflower florets, or celery.

Show off the "new you" at social gatherings when you walk in carrying this crowd-pleaser. You might inspire new DLK recruits!

CLEARANCE CHEETO CHEESE STICKS

TOTAL COST	$7.58
COST PER SERVING	$0.63

NET CARBS

2G

SERVES 12

PER SERVING:

CALORIES	104
FAT	8G
PROTEIN	7G
SODIUM	247MG
FIBER	0G
CARBOHYDRATES	2G
NET CARBS	2G
SUGAR	0G

TIME

PREP TIME:*	2 HOURS
	10 MINUTES
COOK TIME:	8 MINUTES

TIPS & OPTIONS »

Instead of frying all of the cheese sticks at once (like for a party), cook only a few and put the rest back in the freezer.

Be sure not to skip the freezer step or you'll end up with a gooey mess!

Serve with ranch dressing or warm pasta sauce (no-sugar-added) for dipping.

Substitute Cheetos *Flamin' Hot* flavor if you desire for no change in net carbs per serving. One ounce of Cheetos is approximately twenty-one pieces.

Buy short-dated cheese sticks and keep in the freezer to make this easy recipe.

This might just be the most challenging recipe to make in all of *The DIRTY, LAZY, KETO® Dirt Cheap Cookbook*. Does it require hard-to-find ingredients? *Nope.* Complicated cooking steps? *Not that either.* The task before you is much, *much*, more difficult. Here it goes… I'm going to ask you to open a bag of Cheetos (a lunch-sized bag, *but still!*) but not eat a single one. CAN YOU DO IT?!?

⅓ cup grated **Parmesan cheese**

1 tablespoon **ranch dressing mix**

1 (1-ounce) bag **Crunchy Cheese Flavored Snacks, powdered**

⅛ teaspoon **black pepper**

1 large **egg, beaten**

12 whole milk **mozzarella cheese sticks**

2 tablespoons **olive oil**

1 In a large Ziploc bag, combine Parmesan cheese, ranch mix, Cheetos dust, and pepper. Seal and shake.

2 Put beaten egg in a small flat dish.

3 Dip cheese sticks in egg mixture, then add to Ziploc bag of dry spices. Seal bag and shake to coat cheese sticks evenly.

4 Place Ziploc bag of coated cheese sticks in freezer for at least 2 hours.

5 In a large skillet over medium heat, add oil and heat. While frozen, fry six sticks at a time, 1 minute per side, rotating carefully to all four sides until brown, 4 minutes total. Remove from pan immediately. Repeat process with second batch of cheese sticks.

6 Serve warm.

* Includes 2 hours freezer time.

CHAPTER 7

PIZZA

That's a pizza?

I'll eat just about anything covered in melted cheese. Calling it pizza makes it even more attractive. It's all about marketing, you see. I can be convinced to eat healthy food when it's dressed up and labeled properly. Childish? Perhaps. But before you judge too harshly, let me assure you that this strategy works.

Reframing has been one of the most powerful techniques I've used throughout my weight loss journey. By changing the context of a given situation, I'm able to remove cognitive bias. *Whoa.* Did I lose you there? Let me back up. Reframing sounds rather fancy, but it couldn't be simpler. Imagine an ugly painting hanging on the wall. Let's say you're redecorating this room with a new theme, and the colors in this picture don't coordinate with the new look. Instead of buying something new, you can keep the old painting but replace its frame. *Voila!* The old artwork now looks entirely different.

For me, "eating healthy" was that painting I didn't want to look at. Just the words held powerful negative connotations. Because I was always on a diet growing up, I learned to associate "eating healthy" with deprivation and feeling "not good enough." Carrots and celery in my school lunch sack made me feel depressed. I envied my classmates who ate graham crackers or Goldfish crackers for a snack. My Ziploc bag of vegetables felt like a punishment. Truth be told, when no one was looking, *I'd throw them away.*

As an adult with a weight problem, I knew that I had to stop demonizing healthier foods in order to make permanent changes in my life. I needed to reframe this concept into something more positive or my weight loss success would be at risk. Admittedly, this took some time. I had to come up with new jingles and catchy phrases even to sell it to myself. No matter what strategy you use, whether it's reframing or something else, you've got to let go of any feelings of resentment.

> Eating vegetables is the greatest gift you can give yourself. (See? That could be a commercial. Convince yourself!)

These pizza dishes might look a little different from what you're used to. They might even be made from (gasp) vegetables! Top it with pepperoni, sprinkle some cheese on top...do whatever it takes to reframe what pizza previously looked like in your mind.

PENNY WISE PIZZA CRUST

I've been known to use some pretty wild and crazy tricks in the kitchen to incorporate more vegetables into my life. Sometimes my efforts are a hit, but other times they are a complete flop! One time I was trying to make a spaghetti sauce "healthier" by adding puréed (leftover) spinach. *(You could have probably predicted this decision wouldn't end well, right?)* After adding the spinach, the spaghetti sauce turned neon green. Because it was so unexpected, my family refused to eat it. Since then, I've learned to build the excitement beforehand that a meal like Penny Wise Pizza Crust is expected to finish GREEN like the color of money.

1 pound riced broccoli

1 cup shredded whole milk mozzarella cheese

¼ cup grated Parmesan cheese

2 medium eggs, beaten

1 tablespoon Italian seasoning

1 Preheat oven to 400°F. Line a baking sheet with parchment paper.

2 In a large microwave-safe bowl, microwave broccoli 4–5 minutes. Let cool 20–30 minutes and then wring out excess water by wrapping broccoli ball in cheesecloth and squeezing.

3 In a medium bowl, combine mozzarella, Parmesan, eggs, and seasoning. Fold in the broccoli until blended and green dough forms.

4 Using your hands, spread dough on baking sheet in a circle no thicker than ¼".

5 Bake for 15–20 minutes until starting to brown.

6 Your pizza crust is complete and ready to be "finished" in the oven with your preferred sauce and toppings.

TOTAL COST	$4.47
COST PER SERVING	$0.56

NET CARBS

2G

SERVES 8

PER SERVING:	
CALORIES	86
FAT	5G
PROTEIN	7G
SODIUM	175MG
FIBER	2G
CARBOHYDRATES	4G
NET CARBS	2G
SUGAR	1G

TIME

PREP TIME:	15 MINUTES
COOK TIME:	25 MINUTES

TIPS & OPTIONS

Top pizza crust with no-sugar-added marinara sauce, pesto sauce, or Alfredo sauce.

Recommended added seasonings are garlic, basil, and red pepper flakes.

Top your pizza with veggies for added fiber and *fabulousness.*

I consider parchment paper to be an absolute necessity. It completely prevents pizza crust from gluing itself to the pan. I have yet to find an effective substitute.

Reboot a second serving of Penny Wise Pizza Crust as Fortune Alfredo Pizza (see recipe in this chapter) later in the week.

MOOLA MEATZA PIZZA CRUST

✗ ✦

TOTAL COST	$7.80
COST PER SERVING	$1.95

NET CARBS

2G

SERVES 4

PER SERVING:

CALORIES	499
FAT	35G
PROTEIN	34G
SODIUM	942MG
FIBER	0G
CARBOHYDRATES	2G
NET CARBS	2G
SUGAR	1G

TIME

PREP TIME:	5 MINUTES
COOK TIME:	21 MINUTES

TIPS & OPTIONS »

Create a low net carb Fortune Alfredo Pizza (see recipe in this chapter) by using Alfredo sauce and chopped cooked chicken.

Experiment making Moola Meatza Pizza Crust using original, barbecue, or salt-n-pepper flavored pork rinds.

Don't be shocked by the amount of fat generated by the crust. Transfer cooked crust to a paper towel if desired.

Serve with salad mix. Even though it's low-carb, pizza is still easy to overeat. Enjoy every slice with a serving of greens to help "slow your roll."

Pile on veggie pizza toppings! Mushrooms, zucchini, and chopped broccoli bits make terrific add-ons.

When I was on NBC's *Today* show, I made a pizza crust using canned chicken as an ingredient. Al Roker loved the dish and introduced me to the term "meatza"! This go-around, I'm challenged to reinvent the pizza crust with even more creative ingredients. Goodbye white flour, *hello pork rinds!*

2 cups (4 ounces) crushed pork rinds

1 teaspoon red pepper flakes

2 cups shredded Cheddar cheese

3 ounces full-fat cream cheese

2 large eggs, beaten

1   Preheat oven to 375°F. Line a baking sheet with parchment paper.

2   To a food processor, add crushed pork rinds and pepper flakes and pulse 10–20 seconds to make a rough powder of varying sizes of rind bits.

3   In a medium microwave-safe bowl, microwave Cheddar cheese and cream cheese 30 seconds. Stir and microwave another 30 seconds.

4   Stir in beaten eggs and pork rind powder until dough forms.

5   Spread dough on the baking sheet, forming a crust no thicker than ¼".

6   Bake 15–20 minutes until starting to brown.

7   Remove from oven. It is now ready to top with your favorite sauce and toppings.

PAPER PLATE PIZZA

In a pinch, I can "make do" at any pizza party. If wings or salad aren't available to order, I'll survive by eating only the gooey pizza toppings, leaving a depressed pizza crust behind on my paper plate. That's definitely NOT my preferred method as this strategy lacks sufficient amounts of my favorite filler—*vegetables*. When I'm at home, I can be more creative. I can make practically any low-carb vegetable taste like a pizza topping by adding the right ingredients!

1½ pounds cauliflower, chopped into bite-sized florets

1 tablespoon olive oil

½ teaspoon garlic powder

¼ teaspoon salt

⅛ teaspoon black pepper

2 cups no-sugar-added pasta sauce

2½ cups shredded whole milk mozzarella cheese

1 tablespoon Italian seasoning

½ (3½-ounce) package pepperoni

1 Preheat oven to 400°F. Grease a 9" × 12" dish.

2 In a large microwave-safe bowl, microwave cauliflower 4–5 minutes until soft.

3 Stir in oil, garlic powder, salt, and pepper until cauliflower florets are coated. Add to the baking dish and top with even layer of pasta sauce.

4 Add an even layer of cheese on top of sauce and then sprinkle with Italian seasoning. Evenly top with pepperoni.

5 Bake 30 minutes. Cover with foil when cheese starts to brown and return to oven until 30 minutes are up.

6 Let cool and serve warm.

TOTAL COST	$9.75
COST PER SERVING	$1.63

NET CARBS

8G

SERVES 6

PER SERVING:

CALORIES	253
FAT	15G
PROTEIN	15G
SODIUM	968MG
FIBER	4G
CARBOHYDRATES	12G
NET CARBS	8G
SUGAR	5G

TIME

PREP TIME:	10 MINUTES
COOK TIME:	35 MINUTES

TIPS & OPTIONS

When I catch a good sale on cauliflower, this is one of my favorite recipes to make. It's easy to make and an instant crowd-pleaser.

More vegetables can be added to this casserole, like mushrooms, zucchini, green onion, bell pepper, olives, or jalapeño.

Make your pizza casserole a "meat lovers" dish. Any ground meat will be right at home as a topping for this recipe.

My family loves this dish— even my picky-eater son! That just goes to show you that with enough cheese and pepperoni on top, kids will eat just about anything.

NET CARBS

1G

SERVES 12

PER SERVING:
CALORIES	64
FAT	4G
PROTEIN	4G
SODIUM	285MG
FIBER	1G
CARBOHYDRATES	2G
NET CARBS	1G
SUGAR	1G

TIME

PREP TIME:	10 MINUTES
COOK TIME:	18 MINUTES

TIPS & OPTIONS »

Select a wide cut of salami, about 3½" in diameter, to completely fill bottom of muffin cups.

Pay Ya Later Pizza Cups make a terrific party appetizer. They are a big hit with all ages!

Be aware pepperoni styles vary greatly with fat content, which may lead to an excess shedding of fat during baking.

Use a silicone muffin tin for easier cleanup. Sometimes investing in an upgraded kitchen tool can make cooking fun again. I suffered with my old muffin tin for decades before realizing there was a better way!

PAY YA LATER PIZZA CUPS

It's easy to overdo cheese on a keto diet. I'm personally in love with all types and styles of cheese. American or European, shredded, grated, or processed, I don't discriminate. "Come to mama," I say. But because cheese can be caloric and easy to overeat, I make a conscious effort to "slow my roll" around cheesy treats. I do it here by adding leafy green vegetables to each serving of Pay Ya Later Pizza Cups. The spinach greens add necessary fiber and nutrition to my snack, helping me to eat less overall of the *cheesy deliciousness*.

12 slices deli sliced hard salami

1 cup no-sugar-added pasta sauce

1 clove garlic, peeled and minced

1 tablespoon chopped fresh basil

1 cup shredded whole milk mozzarella cheese

1 large jalapeño, deveined, seeded, and finely chopped

6 large black olives, sliced

3 slices pepperoni, cut into quarters

1 (6-ounce) bag fresh baby spinach

1 Preheat oven to 375°F.

2 Push one slice salami into bottom of twelve muffin cups. Bake 7–8 minutes until hardened and starting to brown. Remove from oven.

3 In a small bowl, mix pasta sauce with garlic and basil.

4 Scoop sauce evenly into salami cups. Top with equal amounts of cheese. Decorate with equal amounts of jalapeño, olives, and quarters of pepperoni.

5 Return to oven and bake additional 8–10 minutes to brown and melt cheese.

6 Distribute fresh spinach onto a large serving platter.

7 Let pizza cups cool slightly. Remove from tin using a spoon and serve on top of spinach.

CHARGE AHEAD CHAFFLE PIZZA

X ✦

TOTAL COST	$1.69
COST PER SERVING	$0.85

NET CARBS

2G

SERVES 2

PER SERVING:

CALORIES	221
FAT	15G
PROTEIN	17G
SODIUM	457MG
FIBER	0G
CARBOHYDRATES	2G
NET CARBS	2G
SUGAR	1G

TIME

PREP TIME:	5 MINUTES
COOK TIME:	3½ MINUTES

Early last year, a well-known grocery chain began selling "affordable" 0g net carbs loaves of bread. *Word spread fast!* Without even knowing what the bread tasted like, shoppers filled their carts and emptied their wallets. Store employees couldn't keep up with demand, and thus the Keto Bread Riots of 2019 began. Most furious shoppers left empty-handed but charged ahead to discover a new bread alternative. Through sheer desperation, *the chaffle pizza was born!*

2 large eggs

¾ cup shredded whole milk mozzarella cheese, divided

1 teaspoon Italian seasoning

1 tablespoon no-sugar-added pasta sauce

4 slices small pepperoni

1 large black olive, sliced

1 Lightly grease a waffle maker with nonstick cooking spray and then preheat.

2 In a medium mixing bowl, whisk eggs. Fold in ½ cup cheese and seasoning.

3 Pour mixture into center of each waffle pattern and close (batter will disperse to make two chaffles). Cook 3 minutes.

4 Carefully remove chaffles to a plate using a plastic fork. In the center of one chaffle, spread pasta sauce (but do not go close to the edge). Continue same strategy and distribute remaining cheese, then pepperoni and olives.

5 Top with second chaffle. Return to waffle maker. Close lid only partway (to prevent oozing) and cook an additional 30 seconds.

6 Carefully remove pizza from waffle maker. Cut in half and serve warm.

TIPS & OPTIONS

If you would prefer not to risk facing an "ooze" of ingredients onto your waffle iron, you can skip the final cooking step. Instead, let your pizza sit for a few minutes. The warmth of the bread will warm the insides.

Should any "ooze" occur, allow the spill to keep cooking with the waffle iron on. After a few minutes, any spill will harden, making removal with a plastic fork a breeze.

Make your Charge Ahead Chaffle Pizza "vegetarian-ish" by omitting pepperoni.

FORTUNE ALFREDO PIZZA

Reboot the ATM Pizza Crust in this chapter for a second round of "za." This time, surprise your family with a white sauce pizza á la Fortune Alfredo Pizza! Buying canned white meat chicken and prepared Alfredo sauce is a real time-saver. I buy shredded cheese and riced cauliflower in bulk and freeze. *Bam!* I'm ready to make pizza any day of the week.

4 cups riced cauliflower

½ cup grated Parmesan cheese

2 large eggs, beaten

¼ cup prepared pesto

½ cup prepared Alfredo sauce

¼ teaspoon salt

¼ teaspoon red pepper flakes

1 cup shredded whole milk mozzarella cheese

½ pound boneless, skinless chicken breasts, cooked and chopped

1 cup chopped fresh spinach

½ cup chopped green onion

2 tablespoons cooked and crumbled no-sugar-added bacon

1. Preheat oven to 425°F. Line a round pizza pan (14" in diameter) with parchment paper.

2. In a large microwave-safe bowl, cover and microwave cauliflower 4–5 minutes. Let cool 15 minutes.

3. When cool enough to handle, wrap cauliflower in clean dish towel or cheesecloth. Squeeze out as much moisture as possible. Return cauliflower to bowl.

4. Add Parmesan cheese, eggs, and pesto to bowl. Mix well until a dough forms.

5. Using your hands, evenly distribute dough onto the pizza pan, ensuring dough is no more than ¼" thick.

6. Bake 15–20 minutes until crust is golden brown. Remove pizza crust from oven.

7. Evenly spread Alfredo sauce on crust. Sprinkle with salt and red pepper flakes. Top pizza with remaining ingredients.

8. Return to oven. Bake an additional 5–10 minutes until cheese melts.

9. Slice pizza into eight slices. Serve warm.

TOTAL COST	$9.98
COST PER SERVING	$1.25

NET CARBS

4G

SERVES 8

PER SERVING:

CALORIES	214
FAT	13G
PROTEIN	19G
SODIUM	564MG
FIBER	1G
CARBOHYDRATES	5G
NET CARBS	4G
SUGAR	1G

TIME

PREP TIME:	10 MINUTES
COOK TIME:	35 MINUTES

TIPS & OPTIONS

When adding vegetables as a pizza topping, loosely mix them first with cheese. This combination helps vegetables cook faster.

If a large bag of fresh spinach was purchased for this meal, use remaining portion to assemble a crisp salad to accompany your Fortune Alfredo Pizza.

Expect your pizza crust to be on the softer side. The cauliflower serves as a terrific base, but does not harden the same as other cheese-based keto pizza crust recipes.

Prefer a more classic pizza crust? Reboot the Moola Meatza Pizza Crust or Penny Wise Pizza Crust from this chapter instead.

ATM PIZZA CRUST

TOTAL COST $6.69
COST PER SERVING $0.84

NET CARBS

3G

SERVES 8

PER SERVING:
CALORIES	79
FAT	5G
PROTEIN	5G
SODIUM	215MG
FIBER	1G
CARBOHYDRATES	4G
NET CARBS	3G
SUGAR	1G

TIME

PREP TIME:	10 MINUTES
COOK TIME:	20 MINUTES

TIPS & OPTIONS

To complete your pizza, consider using ½ cup low-carb pasta sauce (recommended brands: Rao's Homemade, Hunt's No-Sugar-Added), followed by whole milk mozzarella cheese and your favorite low-carb vegetables. Some of my favorites are broccoli, mushrooms, or green bell pepper. Mix added vegetables with cheese and bake additional 5–10 minutes (until vegetables are softened and cheese begins to brown).

Double up on the recipe for this crust and save the second one for later use. Reboot the ATM Pizza Crust to make Fortune Alfredo Pizza (see recipe in this chapter).

ATM Pizza Crust fooled even my son, the pickiest eater I know. He absolutely could not believe the crust contained cauliflower. Yes, CAULIFLOWER! My son considers himself a "pizza connoisseur," so his approval meant a lot to me. He has even gone so far as to request that I "make that money pizza again." Money pizza? Because the crust is green, of course! The prepared pesto, purchased from the store, adds just enough color and oil to the crust to make it taste "like a million bucks." *Ba-dum-bump!* Sorry, I couldn't help myself there.

4 cups riced cauliflower
½ cup grated Parmesan cheese
2 large eggs, beaten
¼ cup prepared pesto

1 Preheat oven to 425°F. Line a round pizza pan (14" in diameter) with parchment paper.

2 In a large microwave-safe bowl, cover and microwave cauliflower 4–5 minutes. Let cool 15 minutes.

3 When cool enough to handle, wrap cauliflower in clean dish towel or cheesecloth. Squeeze out as much moisture as possible. Return cauliflower to bowl.

4 Add Parmesan cheese, eggs, and pesto to bowl. Mix well until dough forms.

5 Using your hands, evenly distribute dough onto the pizza pan, ensuring dough is no more than ¼" thick.

6 Bake 10–15 minutes until crust turns golden brown.

7 Remove pizza crust from oven and top with preferred pizza ingredients.

EGGPLANT PAYOUT PIZZA

With DLK you have to think outside the box. Just like how our wardrobe is constantly changing, how we define pizza must stay current. Today's Eggplant Payout Pizza celebrates traditional Italian flavors you aren't used to seeing at Pizza Hut! Reboot Start a Tab Tapas Spread (see Chapter 8) and enjoy a meatless Monday meal in minutes flat.

2 medium eggplants

¼ cup olive oil

1 (10-ounce) bag prewashed spinach

1 tablespoon water

⅓ cup Start a Tab Tapas Spread (see Chapter 8)

1 (4-ounce) package goat cheese, crumbled

½ cup grated Parmesan cheese

1 Slice eggplant lengthwise into ½"-thick steaks.

2 Spread eggplant evenly in a large microwave-safe dish. Microwave on high 4–5 minutes.

3 When cool enough to handle, brush eggplant steaks evenly on both sides with olive oil.

4 On a grill over medium heat, grill eggplant steaks 10 minutes, turning halfway through.

5 In a medium microwave-safe dish, add spinach and water and microwave 1–2 minutes until fully cooked. When cool enough to handle, pour out water.

6 Remove eggplant from grill. Reduce heat to low.

7 Spread equal amounts Start a Tab Tapas Spread on eggplant steaks. Distribute spinach evenly (coverage will be spotty). Top with goat cheese crumbles. Gently return to grill.

8 Close grill cover. Heat 3–5 minutes until cheese is melted.

9 Divide eggplant onto four plates. Top with equal amounts Parmesan cheese. Serve warm.

TOTAL COST	$5.55
COST PER SERVING	$1.39

NET CARBS

10G

SERVES 4

PER SERVING:

CALORIES	393
FAT	29G
PROTEIN	14G
SODIUM	559MG
FIBER	9G
CARBOHYDRATES	19G
NET CARBS	10G
SUGAR	8G

TIME

PREP TIME:	10 MINUTES
COOK TIME:	22 MINUTES

TIPS & OPTIONS

For years, I avoided eggplant because I hated peeling off the skin. I had no idea it was a useless step. Only after I had eggplant served to me at a fancy restaurant *with the skin on* did I finally embrace this purple goddess at home.

Revive near-death eggplant by heavily salting each slice. Let it sit for a couple of hours. The salt draws out excessive moisture, springing the eggplant back to life. Rinse off salt when ready to start cooking.

Sprinkle with red pepper flakes for color and zing.

Serve with Capital Caesar Salad, Extra CROUTONS! (see Chapter 5).

CHAPTER 8

SIDE DISHES

In my "previous life," I turned to rice, pasta, or bread as my "go-to" side dish. These starches were cheap, easy, and always around—not exactly the foundation of a solid relationship! When I changed my relationship with food, I looked for an affordable substitute that wouldn't take long to make. Plus, I needed my side dishes to taste GREAT!

Like most folks trying to lose weight, I've explored most of the available low-carb products on the market. Shirataki noodles, anyone? Only if you like that *eau de fish* smell! *No thanks.* Every so often a new 0g net carbs bread hits the market. I'm always tempted to try a loaf until I see its price tag. Talk about sticker shock! *I'll pass.*

Instead of constantly chasing the low-carb dragon, I have walked away from these products altogether. I'll never be satisfied with those imitations! In place of starchy sides, I embrace a substitute that has yet to let me down: *vegetables!* When dressed up with a healthy fat, vegetable side dishes literally knock my socks off (okay, I might be exaggerating just a little!). But seriously, I love my veggies with all my heart.

I incorporate as many vegetables as possible into my meals. The fiber in vegetable side dishes fills me up quickly and therefore prevents that unladylike behavior of "chowing down" the main dish. Plus, eating vegetables makes me feel good about myself, like a real grown-up!

Let's talk about attitudes, shortcuts, and easy meal prep tips you can use to help you stay on track with DIRTY, LAZY, KETO and side dishes.

PAYDAY PORK FRIED "RICE"

TOTAL COST	$9.71
COST PER SERVING	$1.62

NET CARBS

6G

SERVES 6

PER SERVING:

CALORIES	245
FAT	16G
PROTEIN	16G
SODIUM	469MG
FIBER	4G
CARBOHYDRATES	10G
NET CARBS	6G
SUGAR	3G

TIME

PREP TIME:	10 MINUTES
COOK TIME:	46 MINUTES

TIPS & OPTIONS ≫

Payday Pork Fried "Rice" is what I call a "Bermuda Triangle" for veggies. They *sort of* disappear into the pan. Sneak in near-expired vegetables or those tricky ones your family may not prefer, like mushrooms, jicama, or cooked radishes.

Prefer a vegetarian-"ish" dish? *Hey, that rhymes!* Substitute tofu for the pork and/or eggs.

Fresh ginger root packs a lot of punch. Did you know ginger root keeps fresh in the freezer? I use a cheese grater to shave off only what I need. I've been using the same root for what seems like years.

I'm a big eater, so I'm always trying to create dishes that produce hearty serving sizes. Payday Pork Fried "Rice" technically serves six, but I've been known to eat the whole batch in one afternoon. *Classy!* Not only is this rice-alternative dish healthy, but it's economical too. You can make the meal more robust by rebooting protein from last night's Piggy Bank Pork Chops (see Chapter 9). For added drama, serve Payday Pork Fried "Rice" with chopsticks. I have found that trying to eat with clumsy sticks greatly reduces the quantity of food I am able to eat.

3 tablespoons peanut oil, divided

¼ cup finely chopped green onion

½ medium yellow bell pepper, seeded and chopped

½ cup diced celery

½ cup bite-sized broccoli florets

¼ teaspoon grated fresh ginger

2 tablespoons soy sauce

1½ pounds frozen riced cauliflower, thawed

1 cup leftover Piggy Bank Pork Chops meat, chopped (see Chapter 9)

¼ cup whole peanuts

2 large eggs

1   In a large skillet over medium heat, heat 2 tablespoons oil and sauté green onion, bell pepper, celery, and broccoli with ginger and soy sauce 10–15 minutes until tender. Transfer to a large bowl and cover with plastic wrap.

2   Heat remaining 1 tablespoon oil in the skillet over medium heat. Add cauliflower and cook 10–15 minutes, stirring regularly until softened.

3   Gently fold in cooked vegetables, pork, and peanuts.

4   Crack eggs on top of fried "rice." Gently stir 1 minute to incorporate the eggs.

5   Reduce heat to a simmer and cook, covered, 15 minutes until mixture is thoroughly combined and cooked, stirring regularly.

6   Serve warm.

REDUCED-COST THANKSGIVING RISOTTO

TOTAL COST $8.75
COST PER SERVING $1.46

NET CARBS

3G

SERVES 6

PER SERVING:
CALORIES	167
FAT	12G
PROTEIN	9G
SODIUM	552MG
FIBER	2G
CARBOHYDRATES	5G
NET CARBS	3G
SUGAR	3G

TIME

PREP TIME:	15 MINUTES
COOK TIME:	32 MINUTES

TIPS & OPTIONS ≫

Feeling fancy? Chop fresh mushrooms to start the sauce. If visible, be sure to remove gills from underneath the mushroom caps. *That stuff is just creepy!*

Serve with ham or turkey for the full holiday experience.

You don't have to wait for November to enjoy Reduced-Cost Thanksgiving Risotto. This kind of DLK comfort food is available any month of the year.

Having cozy favorites available like this have helped me "stay on track" with my weight loss for seven years now. I don't feel resentful or like I'm "missing out" on great food!

My family serves a traditional green bean casserole at every holiday dinner. There is something so special about those crunchy fried onions on top! My mushroom risotto alternative reminds me of this popular dish, but without all the carbs. Instead of using cream of mushroom soup as the base, I use a DLK-friendly alternative: cream cheese and broth. I take a few meal prep shortcuts here, even using frozen and canned vegetables. *Gasp!* I can make Reduced-Cost Thanksgiving Risotto before the Macy's Thanksgiving Day Parade goes to its first commercial break.

4 cups riced cauliflower

2 tablespoons unsalted butter

1 (4-ounce) can sliced mushrooms, drained

4 ounces full-fat cream cheese, softened

1 cup chicken broth

¼ teaspoon salt

⅛ teaspoon black pepper

½ cup canned green beans, cut in 1" sections, drained

½ cup cooked bacon bits

1 In a medium microwave-safe bowl, microwave cauliflower 4–5 minutes.

2 In a large frying pan over medium heat, melt butter and then add mushrooms and sauté 5–7 minutes while stirring, until brown. Add cream cheese, broth, salt, and pepper. Stir 5 minutes until melted and mixed well.

3 Slowly add cauliflower and green beans, stirring well to coat evenly.

4 Reduce heat to a simmer and cook covered 15 minutes, stirring regularly.

5 Let cool and serve warm topped with bacon bits.

ZUC MONEYCLIP MEDALLIONS

Sliced zucchini medallions are simple to make and will be gobbled down by the pickiest of eaters. I'm convinced that with enough added ranch dressing, my kids (*oh*, and ME!) will eat just about anything. The best part is that only four ingredients are required. That alone should earn this recipe a gold medal!

2 medium zucchini, thinly sliced into medallions no thicker than ¼"

1 cup superfine blanched almond flour

¾ cup full-fat ranch dressing (*not* fat-free or lite)

¾ cup grated Parmesan cheese

1 Preheat oven to 450°F. Line a baking sheet with foil and grease with nonstick cooking spray.

2 In a sealed 2-gallon Ziploc bag, shake freshly sliced zucchini with almond flour until all zucchini slices are coated.

3 Add ranch dressing to a small bowl and dip both sides of each zucchini slice into ranch, shaking off any excess.

4 Add Parmesan cheese to a medium bowl and press both sides of each zucchini slice into cheese.

5 Place medallions evenly on covered baking sheet.

6 Bake 12–15 minutes until they begin to brown, flipping halfway through.

7 Remove from oven, let cool slightly, and serve.

TOTAL COST	$6.14
COST PER SERVING	$0.77

NET CARBS

2G

SERVES 8

PER SERVING:	
CALORIES	75
FAT	5G
PROTEIN	3G
SODIUM	94MG
FIBER	1G
CARBOHYDRATES	3G
NET CARBS	2G
SUGAR	2G

TIME

PREP TIME:	15 MINUTES
COOK TIME:	15 MINUTES

TIPS & OPTIONS

Zuc Moneyclip Medallions nicely complement a heavy meat dish like Investment Grade Indian Chicken (see Chapter 9).

Cut zucchini into thinner or thicker slices for softer or crispier results.

Have an air fryer? This fun kitchen gadget helps get Zuc Moneyclip Medallions extra crispy.

If crispiness isn't important to you, bake 7–10 minutes and *skip the flip*. The resulting medallions will not be as firm, but they will taste just as great!

RED LOBSTER BARGAIN BISCUITS

TOTAL COST $9.32
COST PER SERVING $0.78

NET CARBS

2G

SERVES 12

PER SERVING:	
CALORIES	226
FAT	17G
PROTEIN	11G
SODIUM	569MG
FIBER	1G
CARBOHYDRATES	3G
NET CARBS	2G
SUGAR	1G

TIME

PREP TIME:	10 MINUTES
COOK TIME:	22 MINUTES

One of my first after-school jobs was working as a hostess at Red Lobster. The pay wasn't great, but the benefits made me feel rich! In between seating guests, I would "help myself" to samples of my favorite Red Lobster Cheddar Bay Biscuits, warm and fresh from the oven. I spent years trying to replicate this flavor in my low-carb kitchen and am proud to share the results with you. The shape of the rolls is different from those at Red Lobster, but the taste can't be beat!

2 cups shredded whole milk mozzarella cheese

6 ounces full-fat cream cheese, softened

¾ cup superfine blanched almond flour

3 large eggs, beaten

2 tablespoons baking powder

¼ teaspoon salt

¼ teaspoon black pepper

¾ teaspoon minced garlic

1½ cups shredded Cheddar cheese

1   Preheat oven to 400°F. Line a baking sheet with parchment paper.

2   In a medium microwave-safe bowl, mix mozzarella and cream cheese together. Microwave 1 minute and then thoroughly stir melted cheeses. Return to microwave and heat an additional 60 seconds.

3   In a separate medium bowl, whisk almond flour, eggs, baking powder, salt, pepper, and garlic together. Add mixture to the bowl with cheeses and stir to combine. Fold Cheddar cheese in with other ingredients.

4   Form dough into ball and place on parchment paper.

5   Cut dough into twelve equal portions and form them into balls. Place on the lined baking sheet with at least 1" between rolls since they will settle when cooking.

6   Bake 15–20 minutes and remove from oven when tops start to brown.

7   They're ready to serve when cooled.

TIPS & OPTIONS

If dough becomes too wet to handle, add 1 teaspoon almond flour. On the flip side, if your dough feels too dry, drizzle in a teaspoon of water to loosen it up.

If the dough is too sticky to handle, refrigerate it 30 minutes and try again.

Jazz up your rolls by adding bacon bits, finely chopped jalapeño, or sliced olives.

For a "prettier" roll, flip and bake an additional 5 minutes. This will make them more presentable.

If your rolls start to ooze together while baking it's *no problemo*. They will taste just as good when cut apart.

NET CARBS

3G

SERVES 8

PER SERVING:

CALORIES	88
FAT	7G
PROTEIN	2G
SODIUM	121MG
FIBER	2G
CARBOHYDRATES	5G
NET CARBS	3G
SUGAR	1G

TIME

PREP TIME:	10 MINUTES
COOK TIME:	20 MINUTES

TIPS & OPTIONS »

I use "Everything" seasoning on, well, *almost everything!* From scrambled eggs to avocado slices, I just can't get enough of this flavorful topping.

I order each of these ingredients online (in bulk) to save money.

It is imperative that all six of the "Everything" seasoning ingredients be as close in size as possible to prevent separation. Avoid using regular table salt here because its small size causes it to separate and filter to the bottom of the seasoning mix.

BOTTOM LINE BROCCOLI WITH "EVERYTHING"

Save time meal prepping by embracing the sheet pan method. Sure, it sounds fancy when you call it a "method," but in reality, I'm sitting on the couch while the sheet pan does all the work. That's my kind of Lazy Keto cooking! Liberally line your sheet pan with an extra-large sheet of aluminum foil for an even cleaner, quicker, finish.

"Everything" Seasoning

½ cup poppy seeds

¼ cup white sesame seeds

¼ cup black sesame seeds

3 tablespoons dried onion flakes

3 tablespoons dried garlic flakes

2 tablespoons coarse sea salt

Broccoli Florets

1 pound broccoli florets, cut into bite-sized pieces

¼ cup olive oil

1   Preheat oven to 425°F. Line a baking sheet with greased foil.

2   In an airtight 2-quart container with lid, combine all "Everything" seasoning ingredients together. With lid secured, shake to evenly combine ingredients.

3   Dispense as needed into smaller 2- to 4-ounce shakers (like recycled and repurposed empty spice bottles). You have now created "Everything" seasoning.

4   To a large mixing bowl, add broccoli, oil, and 2 tablespoons "Everything" seasoning and stir until florets are coated in oil and seasoning.

5   Spread florets evenly on baking sheet.

6   Bake 15–20 minutes until starting to brown. Serve warm.

MOONLIGHTING MASHED JICAMA

Jicama used to confuse me. Is it a fruit or a vegetable? I have seen it play the role of both. It is actually a root vegetable in the bean family. Once you get past the extraordinary skills required to skin it, the magic of jicama is revealed. *It's so versatile!* Because it's such a sturdy plant, you can substitute jicama for apple or potato in recipes. Do you miss French fries or apple crisp? With jicama, anything is possible.

2 pounds raw jicama, peeled and cubed no larger than 1"

2 tablespoons minced garlic

1 cup water

¼ teaspoon salt

¼ teaspoon black pepper

1 cup heavy whipping cream

1 stick unsalted butter, melted

¼ cup fresh parsley

1   Place jicama and garlic on a trivet in the Instant Pot®. Add water to Instant Pot®, close lid, close pressure release, and cook on high pressure 40 minutes.

2   Release pressure for 5 minutes and let cool for another 10 minutes.

3   Preheat oven to 375°F. Grease a 9" × 9" × 2" baking dish.

4   Add cooled jicama, garlic, salt, and pepper to food processor and pulse 1–2 minutes while adding cream and butter until desired consistency.

5   Pour into baking dish and top with parsley. Cook 30 minutes until it starts to brown.

6   Let cool and serve.

TOTAL COST	$6.54
COST PER SERVING	$0.82

NET CARBS

5G

SERVES 8

PER SERVING:	
CALORIES	244
FAT	21G
PROTEIN	2G
SODIUM	90MG
FIBER	5G
CARBOHYDRATES	10G
NET CARBS	5G
SUGAR	3G

TIME

PREP TIME:	10 MINUTES
COOK TIME:	70 MINUTES

TIPS & OPTIONS

This dish is really a blank canvas; you can get really creative with flavors here. What do you think about mixing in a favorite cheese or folding in chopped olives or jalapeños? Let's get wild and crazy with jicama!

Top with jalapeño slices or green onion in place of the parsley.

You can skip the baking step if you don't add too much liquid to the food processor and keep the jicama mixture firm. Just keep adding more cooked jicama and less cream to firm up the mixture in the food processor.

PAYCHECK KIMCHI

TOTAL COST $4.26
COST PER SERVING $0.71

NET CARBS

6G

SERVES 6

PER SERVING:
CALORIES	40
FAT	0G
PROTEIN	2G
SODIUM	585MG
FIBER	4G
CARBOHYDRATES	10G
NET CARBS	6G
SUGAR	5G

TIME

PREP TIME:* 25 HOURS
10 MINUTES
COOK TIME: 0 MINUTES

TIPS & OPTIONS »

During first few days, unscrew jar daily to release pressure.

Paycheck Kimchi gets better with age. If fermented properly, it lasts for months in the fridge.

The ground fresh chili paste called for here is an ingredient I use regularly. It packs tons of flavor with a hint of heat. I buy the Sambal Oelek (Rooster) brand.

For variety, shred the carrots and radishes instead of chopping them. Use a cheese grater and aim for the largest holes. *Watch out for your fingers!*

There is emerging research showing our intestinal "gut" health is closely tied to our overall physical health—your immune system especially. We are what we eat, right? Without getting too "scientifical" about the benefits of probiotics, let me boil it down. Foods rich in probiotics (kimchi, yogurt, fresh sauerkraut, pickles) literally "feed" healthy bacteria in the gut. Balanced intestinal bacteria will reduce overall inflammation. Some say it can even prevent obesity.

2 pounds Napa cabbage

¼ cup salt

1 tablespoon minced garlic

½ tablespoon finely shredded fresh ginger

½ teaspoon 0g net carbs sweetener

¾ cup water

1 tablespoon ground fresh chili paste

1 tablespoon Worcestershire sauce

¼ cup chopped green onion

⅓ cup finely chopped carrots

½ cup finely chopped radishes

1 Chop cabbage into varying bite-sized pieces. Place in a large mixing bowl and top with salt and enough water to cover. Mix thoroughly to coat with salt and let stand for at least 1 hour. This step kills bacteria on cabbage. Place in a colander to drain. Thoroughly rinse salt off by placing in sink and running water through cabbage while tossing with your hands.

2 In a large mixing bowl, combine garlic, ginger, sweetener, water, chili paste, and Worcestershire sauce.

3 Add the green onion, carrots, radishes, and drained cabbage to the spice sauce and stir until cabbage is coated completely.

4 Add resulting kimchi to large canning jars. Pack the kimchi in tightly and fill almost to the top. Make sure all kimchi is covered in sauce. Screw on lid tightly.

5 Keep at room temperature at least 3 days before refrigerating. It is ready to eat after 24 hours.

* *Includes 24 hours of fermentation time and 1 hour brine soak.*

HIDDEN ASSETS STUFFED ROLLS

✕ ◉

TOTAL COST $9.62
COST PER SERVING $1.60

NET CARBS

3G

SERVES 6

PER SERVING:
CALORIES	414
FAT	31G
PROTEIN	22G
SODIUM	557MG
FIBER	3G
CARBOHYDRATES	6G
NET CARBS	3G
SUGAR	2G

TIME

PREP TIME:	10 MINUTES
COOK TIME:	26 MINUTES

TIPS & OPTIONS »

If the dough is too wet or sticky to handle, sprinkle in a small amount of additional almond flour. On the flip side, if your dough becomes too dry or crumbly, drizzle in small amounts of water to reach desired consistency.

Hidden Assets Stuffed Rolls pairs nicely with Swaparoo Spaghetti Casserole (see Chapter 9).

Enjoy with Start a Tab Tapas Spread (see recipe in this chapter) for a savory experience.

Prefer your rolls more vegetarian-"ish"? Instead of pork bacon, substitute vegan bacon-flavored bits.

When you're on a low-carb diet, any smells of warm bread are enough to make your mouth water. Maybe I should just speak for myself, but I admit that making recipes like this get me very excited. Apparently, my happiness is contagious. My kids (and the dog too!) form a flash mob in the kitchen when rolls come out of the oven. I guess they hope that their mom is feeling generous (which I'm usually NOT!). This recipe makes six servings, enough for me, me, me, me, me, *and me*.

2 cups shredded whole milk mozzarella cheese

3 tablespoons full-fat cream cheese

1⅓ cups superfine blanched almond flour

2 medium eggs, whisked

⅛ teaspoon salt

⅛ teaspoon black pepper

1 cup shredded Cheddar cheese

¼ cup bacon bits

¼ cup finely chopped jalapeño

1 Preheat oven to 350°F. Line a baking sheet with parchment paper.

2 In a medium microwave-safe bowl, add mozzarella cheese and cream cheese and microwave 30 seconds. Stir and microwave another 30 seconds.

3 Fold in almond flour, eggs, salt, and pepper.

4 Divide dough into six balls and flatten them on parchment paper.

5 Evenly sprinkle Cheddar cheese, bacon bits, and jalapeño on top of each flattened roll.

6 Form flattened rolls back into round balls so that the cheese, bacon, and jalapeño are in the middle of each roll. Ensure that there is at least 2" separating each roll on the baking sheet due to spreading.

7 Bake for 20–25 minutes until brown on top.

8 Remove from oven and serve warm.

HOMESPUN COCONUT BUTTAH

Instead of buying costly ingredients like MCT oil at the store, make your own! Coconut is rich in medium-chain-triglyceride fats, the quick energy source that jump-starts ketosis. Using ketones (instead of glucose) for the body's fuel source is the fancy-pants explanation why DIRTY, LAZY, KETO recipes make you a lean, fat-burning machine.

3 cups unsweetened shredded coconut

Pulse coconut in food processor at highest speed until desired consistency is reached. Surprisingly, desired Homespun Coconut Buttah consistency can take upward of 10 minutes to be reached at highest speeds, even with the help of this powerful kitchen gadget.

TOTAL COST	$6.48
COST PER SERVING	$0.41

NET CARBS

1G

SERVES 16

PER SERVING:

CALORIES	100
FAT	9G
PROTEIN	1G
SODIUM	0MG
FIBER	3G
CARBOHYDRATES	4G
NET CARBS	1G
SUGAR	1G

TIME

PREP TIME:	10 MINUTES
COOK TIME:	0 MINUTES

TIPS & OPTIONS

If you have trouble getting your coconut butter to "cream up," add 1 or 2 teaspoons of coconut oil.

Use Homespun Coconut Buttah in place of recommended cooking oil throughout *The DIRTY, LAZY, KETO® Dirt Cheap Cookbook*. Keep in mind that, yes, it will carry over a coconut flavor.

Optional additions are unsweetened cocoa powder, 0g net carbs sweetener, salt, and/or vanilla.

Reboot sweetened Homespun Coconut Buttah to top breads like Brown Bag Blueberry Muffins (see Chapter 4).

FRIED MONEY TREE LEAVES

✗ ◉

TOTAL COST	$5.79
COST PER SERVING	$0.72

NET CARBS

2G

SERVES 8

If team DIRTY, LAZY, KETO had a cartoon mascot, I imagine she would look something like a Fried Money Tree Leaf—a slice of avocado for her body, but with a shapely bacon belt...*and pink hair?* Sure, this started out as a recipe, but now I'm thinking this logo could catch on; it might even make a cool T-shirt design. Back when this cookbook was just a pipe dream of mine, my conservative husband (and coauthor) made an offhand comment (or challenge?!?) to get a DLK tattoo if the cookbook went mainstream. Hmmm...I might have to hold him to it!

1 pound no-sugar-added bacon, regular cut (not thick)

3 large avocados, peeled and pitted

¼ teaspoon ground cumin

⅛ teaspoon salt

⅛ teaspoon chili powder

1 Preheat oven to 450°F. Line a baking sheet with greased foil.

2 Cut bacon lengthwise down middle, creating long, skinny strips.

3 Cut each avocado in half down axis, then in half again down axis, creating quarters, and then in half again down axis, creating eight identical wedges per avocado.

4 Wrap each wedge with skinny bacon slice. Place on covered baking sheet, making sure to tuck bacon ends underneath.

5 Sprinkle with seasonings and bake 20 minutes until crispy.

6 Let cool slightly and serve.

PER SERVING:	
CALORIES	192
FAT	15G
PROTEIN	9G
SODIUM	428MG
FIBER	3G
CARBOHYDRATES	5G
NET CARBS	2G
SUGAR	0G

TIME

PREP TIME:	10 MINUTES
COOK TIME:	20 MINUTES

TIPS & OPTIONS

I cook with turkey bacon a lot at my house, but not in my recipe for Fried Money Tree Leaves. In order to achieve the final "crisp," you must use a higher-fat bacon like pork. In this recipe, pork bacon really *snaps*.

Dollop a bit of cream cheese onto these Fried Money Tree Leaves. Yum!

If you like living on the edge with flavors, wrap thin jalapeño slices alongside the avocado. Make certain to remove jalapeño seeds.

When shopping for bacon, avoid brands that advertise maple flavor, as that translates to added sugar. *Um, no thank you.*

TOTAL COST $7.16
COST PER SERVING $1.79

NET CARBS

4G

SERVES 4

PER SERVING:

CALORIES	204
FAT	21G
PROTEIN	1G
SODIUM	703MG
FIBER	1G
CARBOHYDRATES	5G
NET CARBS	4G
SUGAR	2G

TIME

PREP TIME:	5 MINUTES
COOK TIME:	0 MINUTES

TIPS & OPTIONS

Serve as a dip, spread on a sandwich, or use to replace a red pizza sauce.

Reboot Start a Tab Tapas Spread by pairing with any savory bread recipe like Hidden Assets Stuffed Rolls (see recipe in this chapter).

Don't have a food processor? No worries! You can chop and mash these ingredients by hand, *old-school* style!

Not a fan of anchovies? *No problemo.* Omit this ingredient. This recipe is forgiving and can handle switches like using only your favorite olives.

START A TAB TAPAS SPREAD

When I moved into my first apartment (a converted garage!), I discovered the strangest looking fruit growing outside my landlord's door. It was an olive tree! I thought I had hit the gourmet food jackpot until I popped one of those babies into my mouth. DISGUSTING! Apparently, fresh olives must first be "cured" to remove the bitter tasting compound, oleuropein. This was before the Internet (can you imagine?) and I never did figure out how to cure those olives—something I have always regretted.

½ cup pitted Kalamata olives

½ cup pitted green olives

¼ cup chopped sun-dried tomato

2 medium canned anchovies

1 teaspoon minced garlic

2 tablespoons 100% lemon juice, from concentrate

1 tablespoon chopped fresh parsley

⅛ teaspoon salt

⅛ teaspoon black pepper

¼ cup olive oil

1 tablespoon sugar-free pancake syrup

1 To a food processor, add olives, tomato, anchovies, garlic, lemon juice, parsley, salt, and pepper and pulse 1–2 minutes.

2 Add oil and syrup. Pulse 1 more minute until creamy.

3 Ready to serve.

QUARTER COLLECTION CAULIFLOWER

When someone argues that they can't do DLK because they don't like the taste of vegetables, I try to nod my head pensively with a furrowed, empathetic brow. I'm hesitant to share my true opinions with that person, because it will likely be taken the wrong way: "You're right, vegetables don't taste as good as cake." That's SASSY, huh? All of us (including me!) have to face that sad truth. It's like paying the tax man. There is no way around it! Embracing vegetables is the key to losing weight and keeping it off. It's as simple as that.

1 large head cauliflower

¼ cup olive oil

2 teaspoons sriracha sauce

1 tablespoon fresh lemon juice

2 teaspoons minced garlic

2 teaspoons ground cumin

½ tablespoon ground coriander

1 tablespoon Creole seasoning

¼ cup grated Parmesan cheese

1   Preheat oven to 375°F. Grease a 9" × 9" glass baking dish.

2   Remove stem and leaves from cauliflower so head rests stem side down. Place cauliflower head in baking dish.

3   Microwave cauliflower 5 minutes (to kick-start the cooking process).

4   In a medium bowl, whisk all remaining ingredients except Parmesan.

5   Brush oil mixture over entire head of cauliflower, coating evenly.

6   Bake 40–50 minutes with stem side down until cauliflower begins to brown and is cooked throughout.

7   Remove from oven. Let cool.

8   When ready to serve, cut into even quarters and top with cheese.

| TOTAL COST | $5.38 |
| COST PER SERVING | $1.35 |

NET CARBS

8G

SERVES 4

PER SERVING:

CALORIES	208
FAT	15G
PROTEIN	6G
SODIUM	1,277MG
FIBER	5G
CARBOHYDRATES	13G
NET CARBS	8G
SUGAR	5G

TIME

| PREP TIME: | 10 MINUTES |
| COOK TIME: | 55 MINUTES |

TIPS & OPTIONS

One of my favorite Creole seasoning blends is Slap Ya Mama made by Walker & Sons. I picked up a bottle of this during a trip to Louisiana (because of the hilarious name, obviously!) but ended up falling in love with the flavor.

Calling all picky eaters! Exploring different ways of cooking vegetables (roasting, grilling, baking) will help you discover unexpected flavors and potential new favorites. Whatever you do, *don't give up.*

Does a head of cauliflower look like a brain to you? This illusion helps convince me that eating cauliflower will make me smarter.

CHAPTER 9

MAIN DISHES

What's for DINNER?

If I had a dollar for the number of times my spouse or kids asked me, "what's for dinner?", I'd be retired in a beach house on Hawaii by now. Why dinner planning falls only on my lap, I'll never know! Sure, my family all pitches in (albeit with some gentle prodding, *aka screaming*), but I do usually take the lead.

My motivation to create healthy meals for myself and the family is strongest on Mondays. On that day, I'm ready to tackle meal planning with gusto and passion. But if you're anything like me, as the week wears on, you start to care less and less about making dinner (just being honest here!). By Thursday, I consider calling for takeout, and by Friday? *Well*...I might instruct folks to fend for themselves. You can't be supermom 24/7 (or at all).

Dinner shouldn't be so complicated. It wasn't until I learned the benefits of eating leftovers that I finally broke free of these exhaustive meal planning shackles. Combined with the reboot strategy (look for the icon 🔄 in designated recipes!), the use of leftovers enables me to plan a week's meals without feeling so harried. I have better things to do than stress over what to make for dinner! Furthermore, I don't want to be tempted to order food from a restaurant.

> When I cook at home, I feel more in control of the ingredients and the portion sizes I eat.

There is no bread basket or unlimited bowl of tortilla chips to tempt me. The conversation around my kitchen table is much more relaxing than at a hurried restaurant too. The benefits of cooking at home go far beyond cost savings.

Don't let the complexity of the main meal prevent you from eating healthy. One of my favorite sayings is, "Don't let the perfect be the enemy of the good." Stop overthinking it.

FIRE SALE ROASTED RED MASALA

When eating lunch at an Indian restaurant, I make at least two trips (okay, three!) through the buffet line. *"I love me some butter chicken!"* Instead of pouring rich sauces over rice, however, I've learned to fill my plate with shredded lettuce first. The produce helps fill me up and slow down my eating. I love Indian food so much that I'm experimenting more and more with exotic Indian flavors at home in my own kitchen.

¾ cup no-sugar-added tomato sauce

2 tablespoons olive oil

1 teaspoon ground ginger

1 teaspoon garlic powder

½ teaspoon chili powder

¼ teaspoon turmeric powder

¼ teaspoon salt

⅛ teaspoon black pepper

1 medium head cauliflower, chopped into bite-sized florets

8 ounces green beans, cut in 1" sections

1 cup sliced mushrooms

1 cup skinned and chopped eggplant

1 Preheat oven to 375°F. Line a baking sheet with parchment paper.

2 In a large mixing bowl, whisk tomato sauce, oil, ginger, garlic powder, chili powder, turmeric, salt, and pepper.

3 In a large microwave-safe bowl, add vegetables and microwave 4–5 minutes.

4 Stir vegetables into spiced tomato sauce mixture until well coated.

5 Evenly spread vegetables on the baking sheet with no overlapping and bake 20 minutes until starting to brown.

6 Let cool and serve.

| TOTAL COST | $4.60 |
| COST PER SERVING | $0.77 |

NET CARBS

7G

SERVES 6

PER SERVING:

CALORIES	91
FAT	5G
PROTEIN	3G
SODIUM	390MG
FIBER	4G
CARBOHYDRATES	11G
NET CARBS	7G
SUGAR	4G

TIME

| PREP TIME: | 10 MINUTES |
| COOK TIME: | 25 MINUTES |

TIPS & OPTIONS

Optional veggies: sliced green onion and sliced jalapeños.

You can leave the skin on the eggplant to save time and add extra fiber. Or use baby eggplant for a tender skin that is virtually unnoticeable when cooked.

Microwaving the vegetables prior to baking expedites the cook time. This also ensures the tougher vegetables, like the cauliflower, cook fully and soften up.

The eggplant will almost disappear in this dish because it softens quite a bit during cooking and will soak up a lot of sauce. Add more if you like eggplant like I do…*don't let expiring vegetables go to waste.*

CASH OUT CREOLE CATFISH

TOTAL COST $9.86
COST PER SERVING $2.47

NET CARBS

1G

SERVES 4

PER SERVING:

CALORIES	457
FAT	38G
PROTEIN	22G
SODIUM	447MG
FIBER	1G
CARBOHYDRATES	2G
NET CARBS	1G
SUGAR	0G

TIME

PREP TIME:	10 MINUTES
COOK TIME:	14 MINUTES

TIPS & OPTIONS ≫

Fillet size is not really important. Some value brands have smaller fillets, and that is fine as long as you adjust your fry times. Keep the thicknesses below ½".

The cost of this meal can be reduced by opting for lower-cost whitefish (like tilapia or whiting).

Try "blackened" catfish by frying the fillets in a SUPER HOT cast iron skillet using butter. It only takes a few minutes per side. Don't forget to clean your cast iron skillet while it's still hot. If any stubborn bits of fish remain, scour off using a paste of table salt (tablespoon of salt with a dribble of water).

Chefs around the world might cringe at my commentary here, but I love to dip bites of fried fish in mayonnaise. *So crass, I know!* I won't even pretend that what I'm doing is fancy: "Not aioli, ma'am, just mayo!" This habit probably stems from my childhood where I enjoyed munching on TV dinner–style fish sticks while watching *The Love Boat.*

3 tablespoons olive oil

2 large eggs, beaten

½ cup superfine blanched almond flour

¼ cup grated Parmesan cheese

½ tablespoon Creole seasoning

½ teaspoon garlic powder

1 pound catfish fillets

½ cup full-fat mayonnaise

1 In a large skillet over medium heat, warm oil.

2 Add eggs to a medium bowl. In a second medium bowl combine almond flour, cheese, Creole seasoning, and garlic powder.

3 Dip each piece of fish in egg wash (both sides), shaking off extra egg. Then place fish in breading and flip to coat both sides.

4 Fry fish 5–7 minutes on each side until golden brown. Remove to paper towel–lined plate to cool.

5 Serve warm with 2 tablespoons of mayonnaise per serving on the side.

LAYAWAY LAZY MEATBALLS

TOTAL COST $4.55
COST PER SERVING $0.76

NET CARBS

1G

SERVES 6

PER SERVING:
CALORIES   127
FAT   6G
PROTEIN   16G
SODIUM   162MG
FIBER   0G
CARBOHYDRATES   1G
NET CARBS   1G
SUGAR   0G

TIME

PREP TIME: 10 MINUTES
COOK TIME: 30 MINUTES

TIPS & OPTIONS »

I serve Layaway Lazy Meatballs with a teaspoon of Sambal Oelek (Indonesian ground fresh chili paste) on the side.

Steal my "cover pot and simmer" cooking method for all of your future meatball recipes…*genius*. This method also prevents the meatballs from falling apart, which sometimes happens during the flipping method.

Thinking about serving Layaway Lazy Meatballs at your next get-together? Make them easier to eat (and less messy!) by setting each meatball inside a disposable paper cupcake liner. Poke each meatball with a toothpick.

If you're used to making meatballs using bread crumbs, you might be feeling lost entering the low-carb lifestyle. Without panko, how do meatballs hold together? I admit this is a DLK culinary challenge! I've experimented with all sorts of substitute ingredients (pork rinds, flax meal, Parmesan cheese) with varying degrees of success. Surprisingly, I found the "do nothing," lazy man's approach seemed to work just as effectively as these fancy additives. This recipe is so easy you may want to double down or disguise leftovers with reboot recipe partner, Swaparoo Spaghetti Casserole (see recipe in this chapter).

1 pound 93% lean ground beef
1 large egg, beaten
½ tablespoon ranch dressing mix
1 tablespoon unsalted butter
½ cup water
¼ teaspoon beef flavor bouillon

1   In a large mixing bowl, using your hands, mix meat and egg with ranch dressing mix. Form 12–15 similar-sized balls approximately 1" across.

2   In a medium skillet over medium heat, melt butter. Add meatballs and brown all over by frying 10–15 minutes, turning regularly; drain fat if any.

3   Add water and bouillon and bring to a boil. Reduce heat, cover, and simmer 15 minutes.

4   Remove meatballs from skillet and serve warm.

SWAPAROO SPAGHETTI CASSEROLE

↻ ✕ ◉

I used to think Italian food and weight loss were incompatible, like a recovering alcoholic taking a job as a bartender. My armchair relationship with Italian food (up until recently), was limited to what the Domino's delivery man could bring. I knew that if I was going to up my recipe game, though, I would need to climb out of my Barcalounger and get to work. Since then I've discovered the many low net carb compliant Italian flavors at my fingertips: olive oil, anchovies, capers, mushrooms, Parmesan, ricotta, pesto, Alfredo, prosciutto…and don't forget, *red wine!*

1½ pounds 93% lean ground beef

1 tablespoon ranch dressing mix

2 tablespoons olive oil

4 medium zucchini

1 (24-ounce) can no-sugar-added pasta sauce

2 teaspoons Italian seasoning

½ teaspoon minced garlic

1½ cups shredded whole milk mozzarella cheese

1 Preheat oven to 375°F.

2 In a large mixing bowl, using your hands, mix meat with ranch dressing mix. Form 15–20 similar-sized balls.

3 Heat oil in a medium skillet over medium heat. Add meatballs and brown all over by frying 10–15 minutes, turning regularly.

4 Using a julienne peeler, create "zoodles" by "peeling" zucchini lengthwise. Spread zoodles evenly in a greased 9" × 9" × 2" baking dish.

5 Place cooked meatballs on top of zoodles in baking dish.

6 In a medium bowl, whisk together pasta sauce, Italian seasoning, and garlic. Pour sauce evenly on top of meatballs. Sprinkle cheese over entire dish.

7 Bake uncovered 35–40 minutes until top begins to brown. Cover with foil and bake additional 10–15 minutes until fully cooked.

8 Remove from oven and remove foil. Let cool 15 minutes and serve warm.

TOTAL COST	$9.78
COST PER SERVING	$1.63

NET CARBS

8G

SERVES 6

PER SERVING:

CALORIES	352
FAT	17G
PROTEIN	33G
SODIUM	1,017MG
FIBER	5G
CARBOHYDRATES	13G
NET CARBS	8G
SUGAR	7G

TIME

PREP TIME:	15 MINUTES
COOK TIME:	70 MINUTES

TIPS & OPTIONS

Any lean ground meat can be substituted for the ground beef. I often substitute ground turkey instead. Buy what's on sale and stock up your freezer.

A layer of steamed cauliflower florets can replace zoodles if desired.

Hidden Assets Stuffed Rolls (see Chapter 8) would be a great side for this dish.

Save time! Swaparoo Spaghetti Casserole reboots the Layaway Lazy Meatballs from this chapter into a second dinner.

FREEBIE FOOD TRUCK TACOS

TOTAL COST $8.32
COST PER SERVING $2.08

NET CARBS

6G

SERVES 4

As a special treat, sometimes I give myself a little freebie when it comes to cooking dinner. I buy skewered raw shrimp from the deli and then pretend I did all the prep work. My family is always so impressed!

PER SERVING:

CALORIES	224
FAT	11G
PROTEIN	21G
SODIUM	1,032MG
FIBER	17G
CARBOHYDRATES	23G
NET CARBS	6G
SUGAR	0G

1 pound (31–40 per pound size) shrimp, peeled and deveined

Marinade

2½ tablespoons real lime juice

3 tablespoons olive oil

½ tablespoon garlic powder

1 teaspoon chili powder

½ teaspoon ground cumin

⅛ teaspoon salt

⅛ teaspoon black pepper

Salsa

1 large avocado, peeled, pitted, and chopped

1 tablespoon chopped fresh cilantro

2 tablespoons chopped red onion

⅛ teaspoon salt

½ tablespoon olive oil

½ tablespoon water

4 low-carb flour tortillas

TIME

PREP TIME:*	40 MINUTES
COOK TIME:	15 MINUTES

1. In a large mixing bowl, combine the shrimp and marinade ingredients until shrimp is completely coated in spice mix.

2. Cover bowl with plastic wrap and marinate in refrigerator at least 30 minutes, preferably overnight.

3. Preheat grill over low/medium heat.

4. In a medium bowl, combine salsa ingredients except tortillas and stir to mix. Set aside.

5. Give shrimp one last stir to coat and skewer equal number of shrimp on four skewers. Spread shrimp out as much as possible on skewers to allow even cooking.

6. Grill 5–7 minutes until starting to brown. Turn skewers and cook another 5–7 minutes until brown.

7. Warm tortillas on grill for 1 minute, flipping halfway through. Put one tortilla on each plate.

8. Remove shrimp from each skewer onto a separate tortilla. Top each tortilla with ¼ of the salsa. Serve immediately.

* Includes 30 minutes marinating.

TIPS & OPTIONS

If using wooden skewers, soak in a dish of water prior to loading. This prevents the wood from catching fire on the grill.

Prevent your masterpiece from sticking to the grill. Rub the grate with an oil-soaked cloth just prior to laying down the shrimp.

Serve black soybeans on the side for the full taco bar experience. (Black soybeans have 1 gram of net carbs per ½ cup.) I recommend Eden Organic Black Soy Beans.

TOTAL COST	$6.70
COST PER SERVING	$1.68

NET CARBS

1G

SERVES 4

PER SERVING:

CALORIES	258
FAT	15G
PROTEIN	26G
SODIUM	340MG
FIBER	0G
CARBOHYDRATES	1G
NET CARBS	1G
SUGAR	0G

TIME

PREP TIME:	10 MINUTES
COOK TIME:	40 MINUTES

TIPS & OPTIONS ⟫

Deep plates are recommended when pork chops are larger in size. Using oversized dishes to prep makes the process more efficient for dipping and breading. It also prevents a big mess!

To save money and time, I purchase less expensive, thinner pork chops (½"–¾" thick), which have an added benefit of cooking faster.

Be sure to adjust the cooking time if larger chops are used. The USDA recommends cooking pork to an internal temperature of 145°F (followed by a 3-minute rest time).

Reboot leftover pork chop meat in Payday Pork Fried "Rice" (see Chapter 8).

PIGGY BANK PORK CHOPS

↻ ✗ ◉

Does anyone know why pork chops are sold with that weird green jelly packet in the corner? I don't know either! It's a great mystery in my opinion, just like fake grass wrapped up with supermarket sushi. I guess it's all about presentation, right? The lesson we can learn here is the importance of making healthy food "look pretty." We are more likely to eat and enjoy food that is attractively served with bright colors. Piggy Bank Pork Chops look so appealing with a delightful brown crisp. When served with bright green broccoli, the presentation on the plate just *snaps!*

2 large eggs, beaten

½ cup (1 ounce) finely crushed pork rinds

½ cup grated Parmesan cheese

1 teaspoon dried parsley

¼ teaspoon salt

⅛ teaspoon black pepper

1 teaspoon garlic powder

1 pound (approximately ½"–1"–thick) boneless pork chops

1 Preheat oven to 375°F. Line a baking sheet with parchment paper.

2 Add eggs to a large deep plate.

3 In a medium bowl, whisk pork rinds, Parmesan cheese, parsley, salt, pepper, and garlic powder and then spread evenly on a separate large deep plate.

4 Pat pork chops dry and dip both sides in egg wash. Shake off excess egg and then rub both sides in dry breading mix.

5 Place on the baking sheet at least ½" apart and bake 20 minutes until golden and then flip and bake 20 minutes more.

6 Let cool slightly and serve.

TIPS & OPTIONS ≫

Frozen salmon fillets are more affordable than fresh salmon. As always, buy in bulk when possible and freeze remaining fillets.

Recommended add-ons are wasabi and black sesame seeds.

Make your recipe "Hurricane" style by adding cubes of avocado and bits of seaweed.

Refrigerate Supermarket Hoke Poke and remove from fridge when ready to immediately enjoy (to reduce the risk of foodborne illness).

Don't forget the furikake! Pick up a bottle of this potent seasoning at your local Asian market. I bet you will grow to love this as much as the "Everything" seasoning.

SUPERMARKET HOKE POKE

◎

This might offend my family, but eating fresh poke is always the highlight of my summer vacation. I buy this Hawaiian delicacy at the supermarket deli counter by the pound for a fraction of what it would cost to order in a restaurant. For the longest time, I couldn't figure out how to say the word *poke (rhymes with* fillet)—I would silently point at the container with embarrassment. That didn't stop me from going back, though! When topped with a shake of furikake (Japanese spice blend of sesame seeds, seaweed, and sea salt) and a side of avocado, I'm completely full until dinner.

1½ pounds skinless salmon fillets, frozen

2 teaspoons sesame oil

2 tablespoons soy sauce

1 tablespoon finely chopped green onion

1 teaspoon sriracha sauce

¼ cup full-fat mayonnaise

1   Thaw salmon. Dice into cubes no larger than ½".

2   In a medium bowl, whisk remaining ingredients.

3   Stir in salmon until fully coated with sauce.

4   Serve very cold.

INVESTMENT GRADE INDIAN CHICKEN

✕ ◎

Hands down, Indian food is my all-time favorite. From the creamy sauces to the exotic flavors, I love everything about it. Not surprisingly, when my kids were little, they disagreed, preferring chicken nuggets to chicken tikka masala. That hasn't stopped me from trying to indoctrinate them, though! With a steady drumbeat of making Indian dishes, my picky-eater son has finally graduated from eating plain naan bread to entering a new continent of flavors. Investing my time to make these dishes has finally paid off! Investment Grade Indian Chicken finally made the cut and has become a family favorite.

3 tablespoons olive oil, divided

1½ tablespoons minced garlic

1½ teaspoons curry powder

1 teaspoon ground cumin

½ teaspoon salt

½ teaspoon ground coriander

2 tablespoons 100% lemon juice from concentrate

1½ pounds boneless, skinless chicken breasts, cut in strips no wider than ½"

1. In a small mixing bowl, whisk together 2 tablespoons of oil and all remaining ingredients except chicken.

2. To a large Ziploc bag, add chicken and seasoning mixture, pushing out any air before sealing. Knead chicken strips through bag to ensure that they are fully covered with seasonings.

3. Put bag in refrigerator to marinate at least 1 hour. Overnight is preferred.

4. In a large skillet over low-medium heat, heat remaining 1 tablespoon oil.

5. Lay chicken strips out flat in skillet and flip after 10–15 minutes when browned. Cook additional 10–15 minutes until browned on second side.

6. Remove from skillet and serve.

* Includes 1 hour of marinating.

TOTAL COST	$4.08
COST PER SERVING	$0.68

NET CARBS

1G

SERVES 6

PER SERVING:

CALORIES	168
FAT	7G
PROTEIN	26G
SODIUM	140MG
FIBER	0G
CARBOHYDRATES	1G
NET CARBS	1G
SUGAR	0G

TIME

PREP TIME:*	1 HOUR 10 MINUTES
COOK TIME:	30 MINUTES

TIPS & OPTIONS

Serve with a side of Fire Sale Roasted Red Masala (see recipe in this chapter) and a cup of Lotto Chai Latte (see Chapter 10) for the full continental experience.

Explore ethnic grocery stores in your community for discounted exotic spices and sauces. I often find their prices to be more competitive than superstores.

During my weight loss journey I became more and more brave with eating choices. It's like my taste buds finally woke up after a thirty-year nap! Without sugar dampening my palate, I learned to enjoy subtle spices and new flavors from around the world.

LUNCH LINE LASAGNA

One of my unique talents is my inability to give up. Don't laugh, but for years I felt frustrated about my vegetable lasagna recipe. How could I make a healthy lasagna that wasn't so dang watery? I may have finally solved the riddle! In place of vegetable slices like eggplant or zucchini, I layer slices of lunch meat.

1 large egg, beaten

2 cups 4% milkfat cottage cheese

3 cups shredded whole milk mozzarella cheese, divided

1 cup grated Parmesan cheese, divided

2 tablespoons olive oil

¼ teaspoon salt

1 (24-ounce) can no-sugar-added pasta sauce, divided

1 (16-ounce) package thinly sliced oven-roasted deli turkey breast, divided

1 (8-ounce) bag fresh spinach, divided

1 tablespoon finely chopped fresh parsley

1 Preheat oven to 375°F. Grease a 9" × 13" × 3" lasagna pan.

2 In a medium bowl, combine egg, cottage cheese, 2 cups mozzarella cheese, ½ cup Parmesan cheese, olive oil, and salt.

3 Evenly cover bottom of lasagna pan with 1 cup pasta sauce. On top of the sauce, create single layer of sliced turkey, slightly overlapping each piece.

4 Gently spread half of cheese mixture on top of turkey. Then evenly spread half the bag of spinach on top of cheese.

5 Top spinach with an even layer of 1 cup pasta sauce and then create second layer of turkey, slightly overlapping each piece.

6 Top turkey evenly with remaining half of cheese mixture. Spread remaining spinach evenly on top of cheese.

7 Add remaining turkey over spinach, slightly overlapping each piece. Top the turkey layer with remaining pasta sauce.

8 Evenly spread remaining 1 cup mozzarella and ½ cup Parmesan on top of pasta sauce. Sprinkle parsley over top of lasagna.

9 Cover with foil and bake 45 minutes. Let cool 30 minutes covered, then serve.

TOTAL COST	$9.75
COST PER SERVING	$0.81

NET CARBS

7G

SERVES 12

PER SERVING:

CALORIES	240
FAT	12G
PROTEIN	21G
SODIUM	1,154MG
FIBER	2G
CARBOHYDRATES	9G
NET CARBS	7G
SUGAR	5G

TIME

PREP TIME:	15 MINUTES
COOK TIME:	45 MINUTES

TIPS & OPTIONS

Lunch Line Lasagna takes the gold medal for leftovers. There is no "watery" residue in the pan. Finally!

I've been known to use parsley leaves to spell out the letters "DLK" on the top of the lasagna like some kind of birthday cake. *Let's celebrate.* You're eating lasagna and losing weight for cryin' out loud!

Enjoy Lunch Line Lasagna with a fresh Capital Caesar Salad, Extra CROUTONS! (see Chapter 5).

TRADE-IN TEX MEX SKILLET

TOTAL COST $9.75
COST PER SERVING $1.22

NET CARBS

4G

SERVES 8

PER SERVING:

CALORIES	236
FAT	11G
PROTEIN	23G
SODIUM	483MG
FIBER	2G
CARBOHYDRATES	6G
NET CARBS	4G
SUGAR	2G

TIME

PREP TIME:	10 MINUTES
COOK TIME:	40 MINUTES

TIPS & OPTIONS

Suggested toppings are sour cream, sliced avocado, and cilantro.

This is another recipe where you can be creative by adding additional low-carb vegetables like zucchini or asparagus.

Strict Keto folks scowl at using commercial ingredients like taco powder. Sure, you can make your own taco powder from scratch, but who has the time? I'll get to that task right after I'm done churning my own butter from my pet grass-fed cow.

Save time in the kitchen. Use leftovers from Reduced Rate Rosemary Kabobs (see recipe in this chapter) to make this Trade-In Tex Mex Skillet über-fast.

When people ask me, *"What made you start keto?"* I just laugh. I didn't find keto; keto found ME! I didn't have a recipe book or even a list of foods to work with. I figured everything out from scratch with a lot of trial and error (*emphasis on the error!*). Over the years, there were a few ingredients that surprised me by having a higher amount of net carbs than I expected: yellow/white onion, garlic powder, and red bell peppers. When I'm able to, like in this recipe, I trade-in those ingredients for green onion, fresh garlic cloves, and green bell peppers, respectively.

1½ tablespoons unsalted butter

1 pound boneless, skinless chicken breasts, cubed no larger than 1"

½ cup diced green onion

½ cup seeded and diced green bell pepper

1 tablespoon minced garlic

1 pound riced cauliflower

3 tablespoons taco seasoning mix

1 cup chicken broth

2 cups shredded Cheddar cheese

1 In a large skillet over medium heat, melt butter. Stir in chicken, onion, bell pepper, and garlic and cook 10–15 minutes while stirring until vegetables are softened.

2 In a large microwave-safe bowl, microwave cauliflower 4–5 minutes, then add it to skillet.

3 Stir seasoning mix and broth into skillet and let simmer over low heat covered for 20 minutes while stirring to thoroughly mix.

4 Remove from heat and ladle out servings into bowls.

5 Sprinkle with cheese and serve.

HALF PRICE HULI HULI CHICKEN

✕ ◉

Consistently making good choices is important to me, even when I'm on vacation. But eating on the go often causes me anxiety; I'm the first to admit it! I often think about food and worry about menu choices (or lack thereof). I remember one family vacation in Hawaii where my growling stomach led me to pull over and buy a Huli Huli Chicken from a "local" who had set up shop grilling food on his front lawn. I bought the last chicken, slightly burned, for half off. *True story!*

½ cup no-sugar-added ketchup

⅓ cup 0g net carbs brown sugar substitute

½ cup soy sauce

¼ cup apple cider vinegar

2 teaspoons minced garlic

1 teaspoon ground ginger

½ teaspoon red pepper flakes

6 skin-on, bone-in chicken thighs, about 2¼ pounds

1 In a medium bowl, whisk all ingredients together except chicken.

2 In a large Ziploc bag, combine seasoning mixture and chicken, pushing out any air before sealing. Knead bag until thighs are completely coated in seasoning.

3 Let chicken marinate in refrigerator at least 1 hour but overnight is ideal.

4 Preheat oven to 375°F. Line a baking sheet with parchment paper.

5 Arrange thighs on baking sheet skin side up, making sure they don't touch. Bake 40–50 minutes until cooked. Cover with foil if they begin to darken beyond golden before the allotted bake time.

6 Serve warm.

* Includes 1 hour marinating in the refrigerator.

TOTAL COST $7.79
COST PER SERVING $1.30

NET CARBS

2G

SERVES 6

PER SERVING:

CALORIES	255
FAT	10G
PROTEIN	35G
SODIUM	855MG
FIBER	0G
CARBOHYDRATES	7G
NET CARBS	2G
SUGAR	1G
SUGAR ALCOHOL	5.3G

TIME

PREP TIME:*	70 MINUTES
COOK TIME:	50 MINUTES

◀◀ TIPS & OPTIONS

If you are in a hurry, shorten your marinate step to 30 minutes. *I won't tell!*

Drumsticks or breast meat can be substituted for thighs if you prefer without any change in the recipe's directions.

Half Price Huli Huli Chicken serves well with Bottom Line Broccoli with "Everything" (see Chapter 8) on the side.

Is it grill weather where you live? I love to cook outside where cleanup is a breeze. Even if it's the middle of winter, you can sometimes find me flipping meat wearing a parka in the dark.

BIG SPENDER SUSHI

◎

TOTAL COST $7.79
COST PER SERVING $1.95

NET CARBS

2G

SERVES 4

PER SERVING:
CALORIES 140
FAT 10G
PROTEIN 7G
SODIUM 244MG
FIBER 2G
CARBOHYDRATES 4G
NET CARBS 2G
SUGAR 1G

TIME

PREP TIME:* 40 MINUTES
COOK TIME: 0 MINUTES

Don't let appearances fool you. You would never guess that "sushi" could be so easy and *fun* to make. Making Big Spender Sushi feels less like cooking and more like a DLK arts and crafts project. I feel so dang proud of myself for creating these little works of art. This dish is surprisingly affordable compared to what you'd spend at a restaurant. Be prepared for your guests to place takeout orders!

4 ounces cold smoked salmon, thinly sliced

2 ounces full-fat cream cheese, softened

¼ cup shredded cucumber

1 medium avocado, peeled, pitted, and thinly sliced

½ teaspoon black sesame seeds

1 Place large piece of plastic wrap on counter (1½'–2').

2 Lay out salmon on plastic wrap in shape of a square, approximately 9" × 9". Let salmon pieces overlap some but no more than ¼"–½".

3 Spread cream cheese evenly over salmon.

4 Spread cucumber and avocado evenly over 3"-wide strip along side of square closest to you. Space strip about 1" from edge.

5 Carefully roll salmon starting with edge closest to you. Roll tightly so cucumber and avocado end up in middle.

6 Refrigerate 30 minutes to firm.

7 Remove from refrigerator when ready to serve. Unroll plastic wrap and cut roll slowly in ½" rounds.

8 Top with sesame seeds and serve.

* Includes 30 minutes refrigeration time.

TIPS & OPTIONS ≫

Serve Big Spender Sushi with a small dish of soy sauce, sliced ginger, and a dollop of wasabi. It's like being at a restaurant!

For variety, add thinly sliced onion or additional amounts of smoked or raw salmon to inside of roll.

The process of rolling the salmon is much easier if you lift the edge of the plastic wrap to get under the salmon when starting.

Cut the roll with a very sharp knife. Otherwise you will just *smoosh* the salmon roll while trying to cut with your dull knife. Not pretty!

BARGAIN BLT (BACON, LETTUCE, TUNA) SANDWICHES

Pretty food just tastes better, wouldn't you agree? Served on your finest china (which in my case is a chipped platter from Goodwill), Bargain BLT (Bacon, Lettuce, Tuna) Sandwiches are fit to serve the fanciest of guests. Instead of using bread or crackers, this recipe substitutes sturdy cucumber slices as the base of the "sandwich."

2 (5-ounce) cans tuna in oil, flaked and drained

¼ cup finely chopped dill pickle

2 tablespoons finely chopped red onion

1 teaspoon ground paprika

⅛ teaspoon salt

⅛ teaspoon black pepper

1 tablespoon 100% lemon juice from concentrate

½ cup full-fat mayonnaise

2 medium cucumbers

1 cup finely shredded lettuce

8 ounces no-sugar-added bacon, regular cut, cooked and broken into small pieces

1   In a medium bowl, mix together tuna, pickle, onion, paprika, salt, pepper, lemon juice, and mayonnaise.

2   Using a vegetable peeler, create lengthwise stripes on cucumbers, removing every other stripe of skin on each cucumber. Finely chop cucumber peels and add to tuna mixture. Stir and set aside.

3   Slice cucumbers into ¼"-thick rounds.

4   On a decorative platter, lay out cucumber slices. Using a teaspoon, dollop even amounts tuna mixture onto each cucumber slice. Top with equal amounts shredded lettuce. Vertically insert one bacon piece into each open-faced "sandwich."

5   Serve chilled.

TOTAL COST	$6.46
COST PER SERVING	$0.81

NET CARBS

3G

SERVES 8

PER SERVING:

CALORIES	245
FAT	17G
PROTEIN	17G
SODIUM	531MG
FIBER	1G
CARBOHYDRATES	4G
NET CARBS	3G
SUGAR	2G

TIME

PREP TIME:	10 MINUTES
COOK TIME:	0 MINUTES

TIPS & OPTIONS

When selecting cucumbers for this recipe, choose the "fattest" ones you can find. The wider slices provide more space to add the tuna and lettuce.

For a kick, add diced jalapeño to your tuna mixture.

Returning the cucumber skin to the tuna mixture adds more fiber and nutrition while reducing waste.

Reboot a smear of Start a Tab Tapas Spread (see Chapter 8) on each cucumber base before loading to add a salty surprise.

Instead of bacon, insert pieces of rebooted Rent Money 'Roni Chips (see Chapter 6).

OPEN ENROLLMENT EGG ROLL

TOTAL COST	$5.30
COST PER SERVING	$1.33

NET CARBS

4G

SERVES 4

PER SERVING:

CALORIES	176
FAT	4G
PROTEIN	26G
SODIUM	1,248MG
FIBER	2G
CARBOHYDRATES	6G
NET CARBS	4G
SUGAR	2G

TIME

PREP TIME:	10 MINUTES
COOK TIME:	25 MINUTES

TIPS & OPTIONS ⟩⟩

Save time in the kitchen! Purchase prewashed, pre-shredded cabbage.

Since it's being cooked anyway, semi-wilted cabbage springs back to life here.

Experiment with adding additional vegetables like zucchini or mushrooms.

For more protein, crack an egg into the skillet during the last few minutes of cooking.

If including a carrot in this recipe causes you #highcarbvegetableanxiety, omit it. One pesky carrot won't cause you to gain weight, but I don't want you to feel panicked.

Make this vegetarian-"ish" by substituting tofu or peanuts instead of ground pork.

Do you know how to spot my favorite recipes? They're the ones designated with the "I'm Hangry" icon! Seriously, though. I love recipes like Open Enrollment Egg Roll because they really *fill me up*. While cooking the classic Open Enrollment Egg Roll, take a moment to congratulate yourself for everything you have accomplished thus far. What you are doing is brave. Changing your eating habits is hard! *I'm proud of you.* To the tune of "Ghetto Supastar (That is What You Are)" by Pras, sing the substituted phrase, "Keto superstar, that is what you are. Comin' from afar, reachin' for the stars…"

1 pound lean ground pork

¼ cup grated fresh ginger

½ tablespoon minced garlic

2 cups shredded cabbage

½ cup shredded carrot

⅓ cup soy sauce

1 medium green onion, finely chopped

1 In a large nonstick skillet over medium heat, brown pork 10 minutes, stirring regularly. Drain fat.

2 Add remaining ingredients to skillet (except green onion) and cook over medium heat 10–15 minutes while stirring until cabbage and carrots soften.

3 Remove from heat and serve with green onion sprinkled on top.

STASH OF CASH CHICKEN STEW

When the weather starts becoming cold and dreary, I can feel my mood also turn blue. Instinctually, I'll look toward food to feel better. Should I fight the urge? Should I tell myself that it's wrong to fix my mood through eating? My answer is controversial. I have found much more success maintaining my weight loss of 140 pounds by *leaning in* to my habits rather than fighting them. Instead of reaching for Oreos, however, I'll serve myself a steaming bowl of Stash of Cash Chicken Stew *deliciousness* and camp out in front of the TV.

1½ pounds boneless, skinless chicken breasts

2 tablespoons unsalted butter

1 cup green beans, cut in 1" sections

1 cup small broccoli florets

¼ cup diced yellow onion

½ tablespoon minced garlic

¼ teaspoon salt

¼ teaspoon black pepper

⅔ cup heavy whipping cream

2 cups chicken broth

1 teaspoon chicken flavor bouillon

⅛ teaspoon dried rosemary leaves

⅛ teaspoon dried thyme leaves

1 Add chicken to a pressure cooker on the trivet. Add 1 cup of water.

2 Cook chicken in a pressure cooker on high pressure for 30 minutes. Release pressure for 5 minutes and then remove lid. Set aside to cool.

3 In a large saucepan over medium heat, melt butter and cook green beans, broccoli, onion, garlic, salt, and pepper 10 minutes while stirring.

4 Stir cream, broth, bouillon, rosemary, and thyme into the pan.

5 Cube the cooked chicken and stir into pan.

6 Cover and bring to boil. Reduce heat to medium to simmer and cook 30 minutes, stirring regularly.

7 Remove from heat and serve warm.

TOTAL COST	$5.95
COST PER SERVING	$0.74

NET CARBS

2G

SERVES 8

PER SERVING:

CALORIES	218
FAT	12G
PROTEIN	23G
SODIUM	385MG
FIBER	1G
CARBOHYDRATES	3G
NET CARBS	2G
SUGAR	2G

TIME

PREP TIME:	15 MINUTES
COOK TIME:	1 HOUR
	10 MINUTES

TIPS & OPTIONS

Mix and match veggie ingredients to suit personal tastes or availability.

Don't forget about canned or frozen vegetables! Especially with soups and stews, you can save a lot of money at the grocery store when selecting what's on sale.

Whenever chicken broth is called for in a recipe, reboot a leftover portion of Cost Conscious Caveman Soup (see Chapter 5).

If you don't like broccoli or green beans, substitute a vegetable you do enjoy. Make DIRTY, LAZY, KETO work for you. It's flexible!

FIVE SPOT SPICY THAI WINGS

✗ ◉

TOTAL COST	$7.45
COST PER SERVING	$0.93

NET CARBS

1G

SERVES 8

PER SERVING:

CALORIES	206
FAT	16G
PROTEIN	14G
SODIUM	567MG
FIBER	0G
CARBOHYDRATES	1G
NET CARBS	1G
SUGAR	1G

TIME

PREP TIME:	5 MINUTES
COOK TIME:	40 MINUTES

TIPS & OPTIONS ≫

If you prefer your wings dry, and not dripping with sauce, return coated wings to oven for an additional 5 minutes of cook time.

If you like spicy food like I do, then you absolutely MUST keep some Sambal Oelek Ground Fresh Chili Paste on hand. It's more commonly referred to as "rooster" chili paste. It's made by the same company that makes the "rooster" sriracha sauce named as such because of the large rooster in the company's logo.

Five Spot Spicy Thai Wings taste delicious when dipped in a creamy dressing like blue cheese or ranch (doesn't everything?).

What is the best part of the chicken wing…flat or drumette? It's funny how folks decisively land in one camp or the other. Thankfully, my husband and I have opposite tastes in our wing preferences. I don't like to share my food (so embarrassing, I know), so this point is important. Like my dog, Lulu, I might just *growl* if I spot your five fingers coming too close to my plate! Instead of stealing my wings, ask me nicely to make you a fresh batch. This recipe takes just five minutes of prep time.

¼ cup olive oil

1 teaspoon salt

2 pounds chicken wings, separated

⅓ cup ground fresh chili paste

½ teaspoon ground paprika

¼ cup hot water

½ cup finely chopped green onion

1 Preheat oven to 375°F. Line a baking sheet with parchment paper.

2 In a large bowl, mix oil and salt and then stir in wings until coated.

3 Spread wings evenly on the baking sheet and bake 30–40 minutes, flipping after 15 minutes, until done. Let cool 5 minutes.

4 In a separate large bowl, whisk chili paste, paprika, and water together. Add cooked wings and toss to coat.

5 Serve topped with green onion.

CASH ONLY CHILI RELLENO

◉

You've heard me say that I take every opportunity to add vegetables to my recipes. Sadly, not all vegetables are created equal. Take nightshade vegetables, for example. I don't recommend eating potatoes/sweet potatoes (too starchy for DLK), but I do endorse others: tomatoes, peppers, and eggplant. Note that some people experience an inflammatory response to eating nightshade plants. If your arthritis gets worse or you develop a rash for example, cut out nightshade veggies and see if the problem clears up.

1½ pounds boneless, skinless chicken breasts, cooked

2 medium jalapeños, deveined, seeded, and minced

¾ cup seeded and finely chopped green bell pepper

½ cup chopped green onion

¾ teaspoon ground cumin

1 pound chiles, roasted and skinned, sliced in half lengthwise, seeded and deveined

4 large eggs

¼ teaspoon salt

⅛ teaspoon black pepper

½ cup shredded Monterey jack cheese

1 cup shredded Cheddar cheese

1   Preheat oven to 375°F. Grease a 9" × 9" × 2" baking dish.

2   Finely shred chicken and put in a large nonstick skillet over medium heat.

3   Stir in jalapeños, bell pepper, onion, and cumin and cook 10–15 minutes while stirring until vegetables are soft.

4   Evenly layer chile halves in bottom of the baking dish. Add meat and vegetable mixture evenly to dish.

5   In a medium bowl, whisk together eggs, salt, black pepper, and Monterey jack cheese and evenly pour into baking dish. Top with Cheddar cheese.

6   Cover baking dish with foil and bake 40 minutes until cooked throughout.

7   Remove from oven and let cool slightly. Serve warm.

TOTAL COST $8.69
COST PER SERVING $1.09

NET CARBS

6G

SERVES 8

PER SERVING:

CALORIES	274
FAT	11G
PROTEIN	36G
SODIUM	290MG
FIBER	1G
CARBOHYDRATES	7G
NET CARBS	6G
SUGAR	3G

TIME

PREP TIME:	15 MINUTES
COOK TIME:	55 MINUTES

TIPS & OPTIONS

Adjust the vegetables to suit your needs and preferences. Sometimes I enjoy this dish meatless and replace the protein with additional veggies. Spinach, olives, or even zucchini are great adds to consider.

The term *chiles* is a general name for several types of peppers. Your grocery store may not have "chiles" per se, but it probably carries pasilla peppers, poblano peppers, Anaheim peppers, or Hatch peppers. These are all perfectly fine for this recipe. DO NOT substitute jalapeño peppers. They are too small and *too hot* in the quantity needed for this recipe.

REDUCED RATE ROSEMARY KABOBS

TOTAL COST $7.00
COST PER SERVING $0.87

NET CARBS

0G

SERVES 8

PER SERVING:

CALORIES	146
FAT	4G
PROTEIN	27G
SODIUM	72MG
FIBER	0G
CARBOHYDRATES	0G
NET CARBS	0G
SUGAR	0G

TIME

PREP TIME:*   40 MINUTES
COOK TIME: 20 MINUTES

TIPS & OPTIONS 》

Cook more than you need for today's meal to ensure leftovers. *Yes, they are that good!*

If using wooden skewers for grilling, soak them in water at least 1 hour prior to use. Wet skewers won't catch fire during grilling. Better yet, invest in a metal set of skewers.

Avoid having your meat glue to the grates on your grill. Wipe the grilling surface with a well-oiled rag just before placing skewers down to cook.

If barbecuing is out of the question where you live, cook your chicken skewers indoors with a cast iron skillet.

I *realllllllly* wanted to make a few jokes here about *Rosemary's Baby*. I even toyed with the idea of naming the recipe "Rosemary's Baby Kabobs." But that's just *too far*...right? Even though I've tried to improve my barbecuing skills (through the frequent eating of barbecue takeout), I still get an ominous, eerie feeling every time I heat up the Weber. I'm almost certain to burn dinner to a crisp! If you're able to man the grill with more success than I, think about doubling today's recipe and reboot for tomorrow's Trade-In Tex Mex Skillet (see recipe in this chapter).

½ cup olive oil

3 tablespoons Worcestershire sauce

3 tablespoons 100% lemon juice from concentrate

2 tablespoons ranch dressing mix

1 tablespoon dried rosemary

2 pounds boneless, skinless chicken breasts, cubed no larger than 1"

1 In a small bowl, whisk together all ingredients except chicken.

2 Add chicken and marinade to a large Ziploc bag, pushing out any air before sealing. Knead bag until all chicken pieces are coated.

3 Refrigerate bag at least 30 minutes but preferably overnight.

4 Preheat outdoor grill over medium heat.

5 Skewer chicken evenly on eight skewers. Try to space out chicken as best you can to ensure even cooking.

6 Grill 15–20 minutes with grill closed while turning regularly until browned on all sides.

7 Remove and serve on or off of the skewer.

* Includes 30 minutes of marinating.

PESO QUESO CASSEROLE

✗ ◎

While pregnant with my first child, I read every book I could find about childbirth and newborn care. What was my biggest take-away? To cook and freeze plenty of casseroles before having a baby. *Seriously.* I must have been reading the wrong kind of books or was experiencing major anxiety! Either way, I ended up with terrific dinners (*for months*). Even if you're not pregnant, at just pesos per serving, Peso Queso Casserole is an easy-to-make casserole your (or anyone else's) entire family will enjoy.

> 1 pound 93% lean ground beef
> 1 (10-ounce) can diced tomatoes and green chiles
> 1 (10-ounce) bag riced cauliflower
> 1 (1-ounce) packet taco seasoning
> 1 cup shredded Cheddar cheese

1   Preheat oven to 350°F. Grease a 9" × 12" baking dish.

2   In a medium skillet over medium heat, brown beef 15 minutes, stirring regularly. Drain fat.

3   Put beef in a large bowl and stir in remaining ingredients except cheese until blended.

4   Pour into baking dish and top with cheese.

5   Bake 30 minutes until cheese starts to turn golden. Serve.

TOTAL COST	$9.85
COST PER SERVING	$1.23

NET CARBS

3G

SERVES 8

PER SERVING:

CALORIES	162
FAT	7G
PROTEIN	16G
SODIUM	495MG
FIBER	2G
CARBOHYDRATES	5G
NET CARBS	3G
SUGAR	2G

TIME

PREP TIME:	10 MINUTES
COOK TIME:	45 MINUTES

TIPS & OPTIONS

Suggested toppings are sliced avocados, sliced jalapeños, or sliced olives.

To "stretch out" Peso Queso Casserole, I serve each portion atop plates of shredded lettuce. Plus, the shredded lettuce adds another serving of vegetables to my meal. We all know that vegetables are the magical elixir for weight loss!

Commercially purchased taco powder absolutely adds carbs to the meal. Strict Keto followers wouldn't be caught dead with taco powder in their grocery cart! Call me wild and crazy, but I'm willing to take shortcuts like purchasing taco powder to keep my sanity.

STOCKPILE SLIDERS

↻ ✕ ◉ ★

Without Fathead bread to rely on, many a DLK superstar would not have prevailed. Double (or triple!) the quantity of dough here so you can enjoy "bread" with upcoming meals or desserts. Specifically, look forward to rebooting Stockpile Sliders rolls with reboot partner recipes such as Scratch the Egg Fast Salad Sandwich (see Chapter 5) and Lemonade Loot Strawberry Shortcake (see Chapter 10).

2 ounces full-fat cream cheese, softened

6 ounces shredded whole milk mozzarella cheese

1 large egg

½ clove garlic, minced

⅓ cup superfine blanched almond flour

½ tablespoon baking powder

4 ounces shredded Cheddar cheese

4 ounces sliced deli chicken breast

4 (1-gram) slices Cheddar cheese

4 bun-sized pieces iceberg lettuce

½ large ripe tomato, cut into 4 slices

1 In a medium microwave-safe bowl, add cream cheese and mozzarella cheese. Microwave 30 seconds, stir, and microwave again for 30 seconds until fully melted.

2 In another medium bowl, whisk egg, garlic, almond flour, and baking powder.

3 Fold egg mixture thoroughly into cheese bowl. Fold in shredded Cheddar cheese.

4 Form mixture into a large ball and refrigerate 30 minutes to firm up.

5 Preheat oven to 425°F. Cover a baking sheet with greased foil.

6 Remove dough from refrigerator and divide into four even balls.

7 Put balls on baking sheet with 2" in between to account for spreading. Bake 15–20 minutes until browned. Let cool 10 minutes. Slice buns horizontally.

8 Add ¼ of the sliced chicken, 1 slice cheese, ¼ of the lettuce, and 1 slice tomato to each slider. Serve.

* Includes 30 minutes of refrigeration.

RENT-TO-OWN RIBS

◉

Whenever I watch cooking shows, I spend half the time wondering if I have the necessary ingredients, and the rest of the time worried about who will wash all the dishes. I don't have time for all of that! Recipes that don't require using a lot of pots and pans should receive a special gold star. Less mess should become the new standard! Creating Rent-to-Own Ribs doesn't take much fuss. With only five minutes to prepare and a quick two-step cooking method, you'll be licking sauce off your fingers in no time.

3 teaspoons minced garlic

1 teaspoon 0g net carbs sweetener

1 teaspoon paprika

1 teaspoon salt

2½ pounds pork ribs

1 cup water

1 cup sugar-free barbecue sauce

1   In a small bowl, combine garlic, sweetener, paprika, and salt.

2   Dust both sides of ribs with seasoning.

3   Add water to your Instant Pot®. Put ribs into Instant Pot® on trivet, separating to fit if need be. Put on lid, close vent, and cook on high 40 minutes.

4   Preheat oven to 400°F. Line a baking sheet with parchment paper.

5   Release pressure from Instant Pot® and remove lid.

6   Using tongs, remove ribs and place them on the baking sheet. Brush both sides with barbecue sauce.

7   Bake 10–15 minutes to firm up the ribs. Remove from oven when sauce is starting to brown. Serve warm.

| TOTAL COST | $9.64 |
| COST PER SERVING | $1.61 |

NET CARBS

3G

SERVES 6

PER SERVING:

CALORIES	367
FAT	21G
PROTEIN	34G
SODIUM	715MG
FIBER	0G
CARBOHYDRATES	3G
NET CARBS	3G
SUGAR	0G

TIME

| PREP TIME: | 5 MINUTES |
| COOK TIME: | 55 MINUTES |

◀◀ TIPS & OPTIONS

Why are these ribs "cooked again" in the oven? The second step locks in the tenderness. The Instant Pot® thoroughly cooks the ribs, true, but sending them on to the oven provides necessary authentic char while sealing in flavor.

Pork ribs are used because they are smaller and will fit better in the Instant Pot®. Rolling the rack up or separating and stacking the ribs may be required in order to fit them all in the Instant Pot®.

Set out a roll of paper towels and strap on a bib because you'll be getting dirty eating ribs tonight! #dlkstyle

COUPON CABBAGE ROLLS

When I was creating DIRTY, LAZY, KETO, every trip to the supermarket was an adventure. Whenever I discovered a new low-carb favorite, I'd squeal like I just won BINGO. That's how I felt one day when I happened to have a coupon for ricotta cheese, prompting me to read its nutrition label. I brought home a giant container and started cooking. That's how Coupon Cabbage Rolls were born.

1 large head cabbage, cored

1 tablespoon unsalted butter

½ cup chopped green onion

1 medium green bell pepper, seeded and finely sliced

2 tablespoons minced garlic

1 pound 93% lean ground beef

1 (15-ounce) container whole milk ricotta cheese

¼ teaspoon salt

⅛ teaspoon black pepper

1 cup no-sugar-added tomato sauce

½ cup shredded whole milk mozzarella cheese

1 Preheat oven to 375°F. Grease a 9" × 12" × 2" baking dish.

2 In a large stockpot over medium heat, cover cabbage in water (core opening to side) and bring to boil. Reduce heat to medium and let simmer 12–15 minutes while covered. Using tongs, remove outer leaves and place aside. If the leaves feel too stiff to remove, simmer another 10 minutes.

3 In a medium skillet over medium heat, melt butter. Add onion, bell pepper, and garlic and brown 7–10 minutes while stirring.

4 Add beef and cook 15 minutes while stirring. Remove from heat and drain any fat.

5 Fold in ricotta cheese, salt, and pepper until well blended.

6 Scoop ⅓ cup of mixture into center of each cabbage leaf and roll. Place rolls in baking dish and continue until meat filling is gone.

7 Spread thin layer of tomato sauce over rolls and top evenly with mozzarella.

8 Bake covered 35–40 minutes until sauces and cheeses bubble.

9 Remove from oven and let cool. Serve warm.

FREELOADER FAJITAS

✗ ◉

TOTAL COST $8.32
COST PER SERVING $1.39

NET CARBS

5G

SERVES 6

PER SERVING:
CALORIES	303
FAT	16G
PROTEIN	33G
SODIUM	573MG
FIBER	3G
CARBOHYDRATES	8G
NET CARBS	5G
SUGAR	2G

TIME

PREP TIME:	10 MINUTES
COOK TIME:	40 MINUTES

TIPS & OPTIONS ⟫

Optional toppings for Freeloader Fajitas are sour cream, jalapeño, hot sauce, or a squeeze of lime juice.

Instead of a fajita on a plate, serve the dinner with a low-carb tortilla option (try Mission Carb Balance Soft Taco Flour Tortillas, which have 6 grams of net carbs per serving).

Substitute pork, beef, or shrimp instead of the chicken.

Did you know green bell peppers have fewer carbs than the red, yellow, or orange bell peppers? Reduce the carb count by making Freeloader Fajitas with only green bell peppers.

Even though I love to eat, I don't want to spend all day in the kitchen cooking. Eating healthy shouldn't require slaving over a hot stove. In fact, if I could make most of my meals using an Instant Pot® or sheet pan, I'd be one happy camper. Fewer dishes to wash, right? In the time it takes Freeloader Fajitas to cook, you'll have finished a full episode of your favorite show, *commercials included.*

1 (1-ounce) packet taco seasoning mix

¼ cup olive oil

2 pounds boneless, skinless chicken breasts, thinly sliced

½ cup chopped green onion

1½ tablespoons minced garlic

½ cup seeded and sliced green bell pepper

½ cup seeded and sliced red bell pepper

1 large portabella mushroom, sliced

1 tablespoon chopped fresh cilantro

1 medium avocado, peeled, pitted, and cubed

1   Preheat oven to 375°F. Line a baking sheet with parchment paper.

2   In a large bowl, mix taco seasoning and oil. Stir in chicken, onion, garlic, bell peppers, and mushroom until all are thoroughly combined.

3   Spread evenly on baking sheet in thin layer. Bake 30–40 minutes until cooked, flipping halfway through.

4   Evenly distribute cooked mixture onto six plates. Top with even amounts of cilantro and avocado. Serve warm.

CHAPTER 10

DESSERTS AND DRINKS

Do you have a sweet tooth?

I'd be willing to bet that 100 percent of you have experienced a sweet tooth craving. I'm also willing to bet every one of you also felt some *guilt* associated with those urges. The truth is:

> Craving sweets shouldn't be something we are ashamed of.

I hope we can all agree—we are NOT bad people for wanting a dessert!

Even though I've lost 140 pounds, I still crave sweets on a regular basis. Sure, the cravings don't happen as often as they did before, but sometimes, I crave sweets for absolutely no reason. I had to figure out a way to effectively manage my desire for sweets during these instances. Saying "no" to sugary deliciousness is not an acceptable option. *Just sayin'.*

I needed to find substitutes for old favorites that would leave me feeling satisfied. My cravings for sweets will likely never go away. With DIRTY, LAZY, KETO, I'm able to update favorite recipes to healthier versions I can still enjoy. By using low-carb almond flour, rich spices, and/or sugar-free sweeteners, I can reduce the amount of carbs in my beloved dessert recipes. I don't feel deprived or resentful. I have DIRTY, LAZY, KETO options!

I love to bring DIRTY, LAZY, KETO drinks and desserts to social events (without mentioning they are low-carb or sugar-free treats). Can you guess what happens every single time? People LOVE what I bring! Don't look surprised! In my experience, when people hear a dish described as "keto" or "healthy," they tend to make snap judgments about how it will taste *without even trying it*. That's so not cool! I can't wait for you to try these drinks and desserts. You will be blown away by just how delicious, yet healthy, DIRTY, LAZY, KETO treats can be.

CLOSEOUT "APPLE" CRISP

Rhubarb grew in my backyard as a kid. Because of its unique color, I assumed it was some kind of *celery gone wrong*! Stalks grow low to the ground, almost like a weed. If you're trying to find rhubarb at the supermarket, look for the signature lavender color. Surprisingly, the consistency of rhubarb is dense, making it the perfect apple substitute when baked into a crisp.

1 pound frozen sliced rhubarb

¼ cup superfine blanched almond flour

2 tablespoons coconut flour

½ cup 0g net carbs sweetener

2 ounces unsalted butter, cubed

3 tablespoons 0g net carbs brown sugar alternative

½ cup unsweetened flaked coconut

⅛ teaspoon ground cinnamon

1 Preheat oven to 375°F. Grease a 9" × 9" × 2" dish.

2 In a large mixing bowl, combine rhubarb, almond flour, coconut flour, and sweetener. Spread evenly into baking dish.

3 In a food processor, pulse butter and brown sugar alternative 1–2 minutes until mixture forms crumble of desired texture. Briefly pulse in flaked coconut and cinnamon until blended.

4 Spread crumble evenly into baking dish.

5 Bake 30–40 minutes until bubbling and golden on top.

6 Let cool and serve warm.

TOTAL COST	$8.30
COST PER SERVING	$1.38

NET CARBS

4G

SERVES 6

PER SERVING:

CALORIES	167
FAT	13G
PROTEIN	2G
SODIUM	2MG
FIBER	4G
CARBOHYDRATES	22G
NET CARBS	4G
SUGAR	2G
SUGAR ALCOHOL	14G

TIME

PREP TIME:	10 MINUTES
COOK TIME:	40 MINUTES

TIPS & OPTIONS

Serve with a scoop of low-carb vanilla ice cream. Enlightened is my favorite brand!

Be sure to use unsweetened flaked coconut instead of shredded coconut. The shredded coconut is too fine and does not make as good of a crumbled topper.

I buy many specialty items (like baking flours, coffee syrups, and sugar-free sweeteners) at closeout stores. They are worth stopping in regularly to check for new stock. I love a good deal!

You can substitute fresh rhubarb for the frozen. Be sure to slice it in angled slices no more than ½" thick.

PENNY SAVER PEANUT BUTTER PIE

X ◎ 🍃

Did I have you at "peanut butter"? *Yes, ma'am!* I'm a big fan too. But before you get too excited, let's talk honestly about available low-carb options. I'm not sure what the problem is, but every "healthy" peanut butter I try has a consistency like cement. No matter whether I keep it in the fridge or the cupboard, the product *separates into liquid and stone.* Successfully stirring no-sugar-added peanut butter is a serious workout. Be prepared!

TOTAL COST	$9.72
COST PER SERVING	$1.22

NET CARBS

7G

SERVES 8

PER SERVING:	
CALORIES	474
FAT	40G
PROTEIN	12G
SODIUM	202MG
FIBER	5G
CARBOHYDRATES	23G
NET CARBS	7G
SUGAR	4G
SUGAR ALCOHOL	11.25G

TIME

PREP TIME:*	2 HOURS
	10 MINUTES
COOK TIME:	0 MINUTES

Pie Crust

1 cup superfine blanched almond flour

3½ tablespoons 100% cocoa powder

3 tablespoons 0g net carbs sweetener

½ tablespoon pure vanilla extract

2½ tablespoons unsalted butter, softened

Pie Filling

¾ cup no-sugar-added peanut butter, softened

¾ cup 0g net carbs sweetener

1½ (8-ounce) packages full-fat cream cheese, softened

½ tablespoon pure vanilla extract

½ cup heavy whipping cream

¼ teaspoon 100% cocoa powder

1   In a medium bowl, mix all crust ingredients together. Form crust into bottom of a greased 9" pie tin.

2   In a large bowl, combine peanut butter, sweetener, cream cheese, and vanilla and mix with an electric mixer. Pour in cream and mix until blended.

3   Pour filling evenly onto crust and top with sprinkle of cocoa. Chill in refrigerator 2 hours until firm.

4   Cut into slices and serve chilled.

* Includes 2 hours chill time.

TIPS & OPTIONS

Omit cocoa powder in the crust to create a plain Penny Saver Peanut Butter Pie crust.

Top with a dollop of whipped cream. Add a few sugar-free chocolate chips if you dare!

Instead of a glass of carb-heavy milk, enjoy your pie with a cup of unsweetened dairy-alternative milk.

Try drizzling Hershey's Sugar Free Syrup, Genuine Chocolate Flavor over your serving of pie and top with a raspberry and/or mint leaf.

Double the recipe and you have a fancy dessert for that neighborhood get-together this weekend, or just surprise your mother-in-law with a tasty treat.

MAKIN' IT RAIN MASCARPONE

✕ ◉ 🌿

TOTAL COST $7.78
COST PER SERVING $1.95

NET CARBS

9G

SERVES 4

PER SERVING:
CALORIES	211
FAT	16G
PROTEIN	5G
SODIUM	67MG
FIBER	4G
CARBOHYDRATES	13G
NET CARBS	9G
SUGAR	5G

TIME

PREP TIME:	5 MINUTES
COOK TIME:	0 MINUTES

TIPS & OPTIONS ⟫

Don't be fooled by imposters! American cream cheese has less fat (and arguably less flavor) than this Italian superior. Decadent mascarpone is uniquely made from whole cream.

A little goes a long way with mascarpone-rich desserts. If you're serving the mascarpone on its own, consider spooning into shot glasses for a unique, portion-controlled presentation.

For variety, make a chocolate version of Makin' it Rain Mascarpone. In place of sugar-free lemonade drink mix, substitute 100% cocoa powder, pure vanilla extract, and 0g net carbs sweetener.

Some might argue that adding sugar-free drink mix to Italian cream cheese will bastardize its delicate flavor. *They might be right!* Before you report me to organized crime, do me a favor and just take one bite. This rich combination is so heavenly it should be outlawed.

2 cups fresh raspberries

8 ounces mascarpone cheese, softened

2 (3.9-gram) packets sugar-free lemonade drink mix, single serving

1 Distribute raspberries evenly into four dessert bowls.

2 In a medium bowl using electric mixer, blend mascarpone cheese with drink mix.

3 Dollop equal amounts of cheese mixture on top of berry bowls.

4 Serve chilled.

SALVAGED SNICKERING DOODLES

You will laugh at how similar Salvaged Snickering Doodles taste when compared to the "real thing" (snickerdoodles). It's no joke—artificial sweeteners have come a long way! If you don't like the first one you try, be courageous and bake your next recipe using a different brand or blend. There are plenty of choices. Falling in love with a sugar substitute is kind of like dating; you don't want to marry the first prince you kiss.

> 3 ounces (6 tablespoons) unsalted butter, softened
>
> 10 tablespoons 0g net carbs sweetener, divided
>
> ½ teaspoon xanthan gum
>
> 1½ teaspoons ground cinnamon, divided
>
> 1 large egg, beaten
>
> 1 teaspoon baking powder
>
> ⅛ teaspoon salt
>
> ½ tablespoon pure vanilla extract
>
> 2 cups superfine blanched almond flour

1   Preheat oven to 375°F. Line a baking sheet with parchment paper.

2   In a medium bowl, whip butter using a mixer. Fold in 8 tablespoons (½ cup) sweetener, xanthan gum, 1 teaspoon cinnamon, egg, baking powder, salt, and vanilla.

3   Slowly stir in almond flour until dough forms.

4   In a separate medium bowl, stir together remaining 2 tablespoons sweetener with remaining ½ teaspoon cinnamon until well mixed.

5   Scoop out cookie dough with spoon and form into 1" balls. Roll to coat in cinnamon and sweetener mix.

6   Place balls on cookie sheet and flatten with hand to desired thickness. Space cookies ½" apart and bake 12–15 minutes until golden.

7   Let cool and serve.

TOTAL COST	$9.61
COST PER SERVING	$0.80

NET CARBS

2G

SERVES 12

PER SERVING:

CALORIES	184
FAT	16G
PROTEIN	5G
SODIUM	72MG
FIBER	2G
CARBOHYDRATES	9G
NET CARBS	2G
SUGAR	1G
SUGAR ALCOHOL	5G

TIME

PREP TIME:	10 MINUTES
COOK TIME:	15 MINUTES

TIPS & OPTIONS

Salvaged Snickering Doodles come out of the oven in the same shape that they went in, so take pride in forming same-sized balls.

Use a melon baller or tablespoon to measure dough when making balls.

Batches of Salvaged Snickering Doodles freeze well when layered with wax paper. Plan to make extra for the holidays! An assortment of low-carb desserts on a decorative platter makes a wonderful hostess gift. Party guests appreciate a "healthy" option.

GERMAN CHOCOLATE COOKIE DOUGH

✗ ◉ 🌱

TOTAL COST $6.71
COST PER SERVING $0.56

NET CARBS

2G

SERVES 12

PER SERVING:

CALORIES	136
FAT	12G
PROTEIN	2G
SODIUM	33MG
FIBER	2G
CARBOHYDRATES	8G
NET CARBS	2G
SUGAR	1G
SUGAR ALCOHOL	4G

TIME

PREP TIME: 5 MINUTES
COOK TIME: 20 MINUTES

TIPS & OPTIONS »

If the final mixture is still too wet to form balls, fold in an additional teaspoon of almond flour. Or try refrigerating the dough.

German Chocolate Cookie Dough is best enjoyed with a cold glass of unsweetened almond milk.

For uniform-sized cookies, use a melon baller to scoop cookie dough. Perfection!

Freeze leftover portions of German Chocolate Cookie Dough for future sweet tooth snack attacks. Separate cookies using layers of wax paper or inside individually portioned Ziploc bags.

Plan to double or triple this recipe. *Oh yeah, it's that good!*

Do you think most of our "food issues" stem from our childhood? For me, I'd say that's very likely. Whether good or bad, I was raised in a household that celebrated *every* special occasion with food. Got a new job? *Let's go out to dinner.* All A's on your report card? *Here's a cookie!* Birthdays ranked the highest for food celebrations. Growing up, we always picked sweets for Mom to bake for these special moments. My dad's favorite cookie was made with chocolate, pecans, and coconut. My German Chocolate Cookie Dough recipe is a throwback to this unique dessert. *This one's for you, Dad!*

¼ cup superfine blanched almond flour

3 tablespoons 100% cocoa powder

1 teaspoon dry coffee grounds

½ cup 0g net carbs sweetener

⅛ teaspoon salt

3 tablespoons unsalted butter, melted

⅓ cup heavy whipping cream

½ teaspoon pure vanilla extract

1 large egg, beaten

1 cup shredded unsweetened coconut

¼ cup finely chopped pecans

1   Preheat oven to 350°F. Line a baking sheet with parchment paper.

2   In a medium bowl, combine almond flour, cocoa, coffee, sweetener, and salt. Add remaining ingredients and stir to mix until dough forms.

3   Form dough into 1"–1½" balls and place on the baking sheet. Flatten to desired thickness and separate by at least ½".

4   Bake 15–20 minutes until toothpick inserted into the center comes out dry.

5   Serve warm.

CONVENIENCE STORE CANDY ALMONDS

Every February, the rural landscape surrounding my house blossoms into awe-inspiring fields of pink. Even though it's winter, Cupid tells the blossoms that it's time to pollinate and populate! I live in "a-min" country, you see. Most of the world's "a-mins" grow on trees from my hometown. You can trust my legit pronunciation of what *y'all* like to call almonds.

8 ounces whole almonds

1 tablespoon unsalted butter, melted

1 tablespoon 100% cocoa powder

4 tablespoons 0g net carbs sweetener

⅛ teaspoon salt

⅛ teaspoon cayenne pepper

1 Preheat oven to 375°F. Line a baking sheet with parchment paper.

2 Spread almonds on baking sheet in single layer.

3 Toast almonds in oven 10–15 minutes, turning almonds halfway through cooking time.

4 In a medium bowl, combine hot toasted almonds with melted butter and stir to coat.

5 In a medium bowl, thoroughly mix cocoa, sweetener, salt, and cayenne pepper. Add buttery nuts to dry mix and stir to evenly coat.

6 Return single layer of chocolate-covered almonds to the baking sheet and bake additional 7 minutes, stirring once.

7 Let cool before eating. Coating will harden as it cools.

TOTAL COST	$3.97
COST PER SERVING	$0.50

NET CARBS

3G

SERVES 8

PER SERVING:

CALORIES	181
FAT	15G
PROTEIN	6G
SODIUM	36MG
FIBER	4G
CARBOHYDRATES	10G
NET CARBS	3G
SUGAR	1G
SUGAR ALCOHOL	3G

TIME

PREP TIME:	5 MINUTES
COOK TIME:	22 MINUTES

TIPS & OPTIONS

Monitor your toasting almonds carefully. They can burn in the blink of an eye. I stand guard during the toasting process—plus, the smell of toasting nuts is fantastic!

Once cool, portion Convenience Store Candy Almonds into eight Ziploc bags. This helps prevent eating the entire batch at once!

Store (hide) Convenience Store Candy Almonds in the freezer for future enjoyment.

The hardest step is the last. I ALWAYS forget to wait, popping a scorching hot almond into my mouth, which burns the bejesus out of my tongue. It's just embarrassing, really.

NET CARBS

4G

SERVES 8

PER SERVING:

CALORIES	297
FAT	25G
PROTEIN	8G
SODIUM	143MG
FIBER	5G
CARBOHYDRATES	12G
NET CARBS	4G
SUGAR	2G
SUGAR ALCOHOL	3G

TIME

PREP TIME:	10 MINUTES
COOK TIME:	30 MINUTES

TIPS & OPTIONS ≫

Suggested added ingredients are sugar-free chocolate chips and chopped walnuts.

Top with a dollop of whipped cream or serving of frozen regular Cool Whip (not lite).

I definitely recommend investing in a few pressure cooker accessories right away. A muffin tin, cake pans, and a steamer basket will come in handy. Select accessories that have a sturdy handle. This helps you carefully remove heavy or awkward items without burning yourself.

Coffee, salt, and cayenne pepper add more depth to chocolate recipes. Experiment with these ingredients for a surprising, rich result.

CHA-CHING CHOCOLATE PUDDIN' CAKE

I have a long history of making baked goods that never reached the oven. I would make the batter with the best intentions, I swear! I will even admit to reaching inside the oven with a spoon for "one last bite" of batter. Surely, I'm not the only one that has done this? That's why I transitioned over to the Instant Pot® for cake making. This pressure cooker Cha-Ching Chocolate Puddin' Cake literally goes on "lockdown" to cook, keeping sticky fingers like mine at bay.

1 cup superfine blanched almond flour

⅓ cup coconut flour

½ cup 100% cocoa powder

4 tablespoons 0g net carbs sweetener

1½ teaspoons baking powder

1 cup unsweetened canned coconut milk

1 (4-ounce) stick unsalted butter, melted

1 teaspoon pure vanilla extract

4 medium eggs, beaten

1 In a medium bowl, whisk almond flour, coconut flour, cocoa powder, sweetener, and baking powder to combine.

2 Whisk in remaining ingredients until thoroughly blended.

3 Spray baking pan that will fit in your pressure cooker with nonstick cooking spray.

4 Add batter and cover baking pan with foil.

5 Add 1 cup water to bottom of pressure cooker and place baking pan in cooker on top of trivet.

6 Close lid, close vent, and cook on high pressure 30 minutes.

7 Release pressure and remove lid. When cool enough to handle, remove cake and remove foil.

8 Serve warm.

NO SHARING CHOCOLATE PEANUT BUTTER "CUP" CAKE

✕ 🌿

Some desserts are best enjoyed in small quantities. Which ones, you ask? Well, the ones that are so good that you can't control yourself! I've been known to eat an entire low-carb cheesecake, all by myself, in just under 24 hours. The struggle is real! Because I recognize the limits of my willpower, I prefer to make desserts in small or single portion sizes. This No Sharing Chocolate Peanut Butter "Cup" Cake is a great example of a single portion dessert that won't get you in (too much) trouble.

> 2 tablespoons no-sugar-added peanut butter
>
> 3 (1-gram) packets 0g net carbs sweetener
>
> 1 large egg, beaten
>
> ¼ teaspoon baking powder
>
> 1 tablespoon sugar-free chocolate chips

1 Spray a medium microwave-safe coffee mug with nonstick cooking spray.

2 Add peanut butter. Microwave 45–60 seconds to soften.

3 Add remaining ingredients and stir to mix well.

4 Microwave 60 seconds.

5 Serve warm.

TOTAL COST	$1.02
COST PER SERVING	$1.02

NET CARBS

7G

SERVES 1

PER SERVING:	
CALORIES	304
FAT	24G
PROTEIN	15G
SODIUM	247MG
FIBER	7G
CARBOHYDRATES	20G
NET CARBS	7G
SUGAR	2G
SUGAR ALCOHOL	6G

TIME

PREP TIME:	5 MINUTES
COOK TIME:	2 MINUTES

« TIPS & OPTIONS

For added awesomeness, top your cake with a dollop of whipped cream.

Because no-sugar-added peanut butter often comes at a hefty price, I often enjoy the "regular stuff." Sure, it might have a few more net carbs per serving, but sometimes I'm willing to make it work in the big picture of my daily carb count in the name of convenience.

I recently discovered Great Value Organic Peanut Butter with only 1 gram of net carbs per serving. Wow!

Another option to consider is to create homemade peanut butter. Blend peanuts in a food processor.

LEMONADE LOOT STRAWBERRY SHORTCAKE

TOTAL COST $5.43
COST PER SERVING $1.36

NET CARBS

10G

SERVES 4

PER SERVING:

CALORIES	298
FAT	21G
PROTEIN	14G
SODIUM	708MG
FIBER	2G
CARBOHYDRATES	13G
NET CARBS	10G
SUGAR	3G
SUGAR ALCOHOL	1G

TIME

PREP TIME:* 40 MINUTES
COOK TIME: 21 MINUTES

TIPS & OPTIONS

Give your "cake" a more traditional flavor by substituting the lemonade flavored drink mix with ¼ teaspoon vanilla.

Add color *and pizazz* to the cake by substituting 1 teaspoon of your favorite flavor of sugar-free gelatin mix instead of the lemonade drink mix and slightly reduce bake time to 13–15 minutes.

For an alternative to this cheese-based shortcake, try making traditional biscuits using Carbquik brand baking mix (recipe on side of box). Carbquik is available online, and occasionally on the shelf at superstores. This clever ingredient is worth the hassle and expense.

Lemonade Loot Strawberry Shortcake *almost* reboots the Stockpile Sliders bread (see Chapter 9), but with a late-stage tropical twist. By introducing a few tweaks like a single serving packet of sugar-free lemonade drink mix to the dough, Stockpile Sliders buns transform into dense lemon shortcake!

Shortcake

2 ounces full-fat cream cheese, softened

6 ounces shredded whole milk mozzarella cheese

1 large egg, beaten

1 (3.9-gram) packet sugar-free lemonade drink mix, single serving

⅓ cup superfine blanched almond flour

4 (1-gram) packets 0g net carbs sweetener

1 tablespoon baking powder

Topping

1 cup chopped fresh strawberries

3 tablespoons no-sugar-added red raspberry jam

8 tablespoons canned unsweetened whipped cream

1 In a medium microwave-safe bowl, add cream cheese and mozzarella cheese. Microwave 30 seconds and stir. Repeat.

2 In a large bowl, whisk together remaining shortcake ingredients.

3 Combine cheeses with the shortcake ingredients and mix well.

4 Form resulting dough into a large ball and refrigerate 30 minutes.

5 Preheat oven to 425°F. Cover a baking sheet with greased foil.

6 In a small bowl, add strawberries and jam. Gently stir to evenly coat berries. Set aside.

7 Remove dough from refrigerator and divide into four even balls.

8 Put balls on the baking sheet with 2" in between to account for spreading.

9 Bake 15–20 minutes until browned. Let cool 10 minutes.

10 Place buns into four bowls and top evenly with strawberry mixture and whipped cream. Serve chilled.

* Includes 30 minutes of setup time in the fridge.

GARAGE SALE BLOWTORCH CRÈME BRÛLÉE

✗ ◉ 🌱

One of my favorite *DIRTY, LAZY, Girl* podcast recordings was about kitchen hoarding. I admitted to having a coffin-sized freezer overstocked with so much frozen food I didn't know what was buried at the bottom. My cohost, Tamara, revealed she could barely park in her garage because of a growing kitchen appliance boneyard hogging so much space! Out of everyone I know, I bet Tamara has a handheld *kitchen* blowtorch in her garage I could borrow to properly finish off my crème brûlée.

2 large egg yolks, beaten

½ teaspoon pure vanilla extract

1 cup heavy whipping cream

¼ cup 0g net carbs sweetener

⅛ teaspoon salt

1 tablespoon 0g net carbs brown sugar substitute

1   Preheat oven to 350°F. Insert silicone liners into muffin tin cups.

2   In a small bowl, whisk egg yolks and vanilla together.

3   To a medium saucepan over medium heat, add cream, sweetener, and salt. Bring to boil and then immediately remove from heat while stirring to combine and dissolve sweetener and salt.

4   Slowly stir in yolk mixture and whisk until thoroughly combined. Pour mixture evenly into muffin cups.

5   Bake 20–25 minutes until baked throughout.

6   Remove from oven and top evenly with brown sugar substitute.

7   Preheat oven broiler on high.

8   Briefly place muffin cups under broiler, 1–2 minutes, until top layer browns and becomes hard. *Monitor this last step carefully to prevent burning.*

9   Let cool slightly and serve (while still in liner).

TOTAL COST	$4.90
COST PER SERVING	$0.82

NET CARBS

1G

SERVES 6

PER SERVING:

CALORIES	160
FAT	15G
PROTEIN	2G
SODIUM	66MG
FIBER	0G
CARBOHYDRATES	6G
NET CARBS	1G
SUGAR	1G
SUGAR ALCOHOL	5G

TIME

PREP TIME:	10 MINUTES
COOK TIME:	27 MINUTES

TIPS & OPTIONS

If you happen to have a handheld kitchen blowtorch *(that's so random!)*, you're in luck. This is your gold star opportunity to *reallllllllly* get fired up. Skip the "under the broiler" step and use your trusty kitchen gadget instead. *Hot stuff!* Plus, you'll look really cool in front of your family.

When it's time to distribute the batter into the muffin tins, transfer the batter first from the mixing bowl into a large glass measuring cup. This added step (and dish to wash—*sad!*) proves worthwhile. You'll gain more control of the batter, which ultimately results in evenly-sized cups.

BARGAIN BASEMENT COFFEE CAKE BITES

TOTAL COST $7.62
COST PER SERVING $0.76

NET CARBS

3G

SERVES 10

PER SERVING:

CALORIES	164
FAT	13G
PROTEIN	5G
SODIUM	126MG
FIBER	2G
CARBOHYDRATES	11G
NET CARBS	3G
SUGAR	1G
SUGAR ALCOHOL	6.4G

TIME

PREP TIME:	10 MINUTES
COOK TIME:	20 MINUTES

TIPS & OPTIONS ≫

Additional toppings could be sugar-free chocolate chips or chopped nuts.

Enjoy with a spread of Homespun Coconut Buttah (see Chapter 8). The added fat will keep you feeling fuller, for longer.

Do Bargain Basement Coffee Cake Bites only belong in the dessert category? *No siree!* I sometimes enjoy this treat for breakfast too.

If you're like me and have trouble stopping after just one serving of baked goods, consider reserving these types of recipes only for special occasions.

The coffee shop habit is hard to break. I have many friends that go once (if not twice!) a day for a quick pick-me-up. Instead of using food to reward yourself, can I suggest taking a walk instead? I know, I know, that sounds ridiculous… Exercise instead of COFFEE AND CAKE? Yes, I've become *that* person! Let's take this one step at a time. Baby steps! Enjoy a gourmet coffee, but bring your own bites of DIRTY, LAZY, KETO Bargain Basement Coffee Cake Bites.

1½ cups superfine blanched almond flour

⅔ cup 0g net carbs sweetener, divided

1 teaspoon baking powder

¼ teaspoon salt

2 large eggs

3 tablespoons unsalted butter, softened, divided

1 teaspoon pure vanilla extract

¼ cup unsweetened almond milk

1½ tablespoons ground cinnamon

1 Preheat oven to 375°F. Grease a large muffin tin.

2 In a medium bowl, whisk almond flour, ⅓ cup sweetener, baking powder, and salt.

3 Add eggs, 2 tablespoons butter, vanilla, and almond milk and fold until well mixed.

4 In a separate medium bowl, combine 1 tablespoon butter, cinnamon, and ⅓ cup sweetener.

5 Fill ten cups of the muffin tin about ⅓ full with almond flour batter. Add approximately 2 teaspoons of cinnamon batter and top with a large dollop of almond flour batter that is equal to about ⅓ of muffin cup.

6 Bake 15–20 minutes until a toothpick inserted into the center comes out clean. Serve warm.

COMPLIMENTARY DINNER MINT SMOOTHIE

TOTAL COST	$6.69
COST PER SERVING	$3.35

NET CARBS

5G

SERVES 2

PER SERVING:

CALORIES	285
FAT	24G
PROTEIN	9G
SODIUM	188MG
FIBER	4G
CARBOHYDRATES	9G
NET CARBS	5G
SUGAR	2G

TIME

PREP TIME:	10 MINUTES
COOK TIME:	0 MINUTES

TIPS & OPTIONS »

I'm always on the lookout for sneaky ways to add healthy ingredients to meals. Smoothies allow me this flexibility.

Avoid fat-free yogurt! Recipes from *The DIRTY, LAZY, KETO® Dirt Cheap Cookbook* need fat for flavor and to keep you feeling fuller for longer. Choose yogurt 2–5 percent fat or higher with net carbs totaling 2–8 grams per serving.

Be aware of the serving size on the yogurt's nutrition label. I have discovered there is no universal serving size among competing brands; serving sizes vary from ½ cup to ⅔ cup all the way up to 1 cup. *Shop wisely!*

I have a friend that complains about having to eat at a restaurant every day for lunch (I don't know about you, but that sounds heavenly to me!). I try to empathize with her (really, I do!), as I can see how that habit might lead to overeating. Serving sizes at restaurants do tend to be larger than what we would serve ourselves. Instead of making a fancy-pants dinner, my friend likes to enjoy a low-stress meal like the Complimentary Dinner Mint Smoothie.

1 cup ice

1 cup unsweetened almond milk

½ cup full-fat plain Greek yogurt

½ cup unsweetened canned coconut milk

½ medium avocado, peeled and pitted

½ cup chopped fresh mint

1 cup chopped fresh spinach

1 cup chopped fresh kale

4 (1-gram) packets 0g net carbs sweetener

1 In a large blender, pulse all ingredients at once until desired consistency is reached.

2 Pour into two pint glasses and enjoy with a friend.

HOT "TO TROT" TAX TODDY

When you eat fewer carbs, the effects of alcohol are more taxing to your system. You might even discover your tolerance has dramatically decreased! Take note of how your body responds to alcohol. If you start acting "hot to trot," you may need to "slow your roll"! *Drink responsibly.*

6 ounces hot tea, brewed

1½ ounces unflavored whiskey

¾ tablespoon fresh lemon juice

⅛" slice fresh ginger, peeled

½ tablespoon unsalted butter, melted

2 (1-gram) packets 0g net carbs sweetener

1 cinnamon stick

1   Put tea in your favorite mug or handled glass.

2   Add whiskey, lemon juice, ginger slice, and butter.

3   Stir in sweetener with cinnamon stick and enjoy. Leave cinnamon stick in cup.

TOTAL COST	$1.58
COST PER SERVING	$1.58

NET CARBS

1G

SERVES 1

PER SERVING:

CALORIES	125
FAT	2G
PROTEIN	0G
SODIUM	5MG
FIBER	0G
CARBOHYDRATES	1G
NET CARBS	1G
SUGAR	0G

TIME

PREP TIME:	5 MINUTES
COOK TIME:	0 MINUTES

TIPS & OPTIONS

A 0 grams net carbs syrup would also work as a sweetener in this recipe.

A glass cup with a handle is preferred for this recipe so you can see and enjoy the exotic ingredients. Be sure it's a hot temperature–safe glass, though!

As a reminder, unflavored hard alcohols have 0 grams of net carbs per 1½ fluid ounce shot serving.

Dress up your cocktail with a citrus slice garnish hooked on the rim of the glass.

Hot "to Trot" Tax Toddy isn't just for special occasions— toast the town any day of the week. It hits the spot and *warms the soul.*

WONDER IF I WON EGGNOG

TOTAL COST $8.22
COST PER SERVING $1.37

NET CARBS

3G

SERVES 6

PER SERVING:
CALORIES	367
FAT	24G
PROTEIN	8G
SODIUM	240MG
FIBER	1G
CARBOHYDRATES	12G
NET CARBS	3G
SUGAR	2G
SUGAR ALCOHOL	8G

TIME

PREP TIME:*	4 HOURS 10 MINUTES
COOK TIME:	22 MINUTES

One of the most celebrated moments in the DIRTY, LAZY, KETO journey occurs when you enter the gates of "one-derland." This happens when the scale shows number one as the first number. For many of us, that hasn't happened in a *reallllllllly* long time. When I lost enough weight to enter the "one-hundreds," I remember crying tears of happiness in the bathroom while simultaneously trying to take a picture of the scale. Sadly, every time I picked up my phone (to use the camera), the increased weight caused the scale to flip back into the twos again. *Errr!*

5 cups unsweetened almond milk

1¼ cups heavy whipping cream

1 teaspoon ground nutmeg

2 teaspoons ground cinnamon, divided

6 large eggs

1 cup 0g net carbs sweetener

1½ teaspoons pure vanilla extract

1 cup white rum

1   In a large pot over medium heat, add almond milk, heavy cream, nutmeg, and most of cinnamon, leaving a bit for garnish. Heat 12 minutes, constantly stirring. DO NOT bring liquid to a boil.

2   In a medium bowl, whisk together eggs and sweetener.

3   Slowly whisk 1 cup of very hot dairy mixture into egg mixture to temper it and prevent curdling.

4   Slowly stir tempered egg mixture with dairy mixture in pan. Stir constantly and bring close to a boil, about 5 minutes.

5   Remove mixture from heat and pour into medium metal mixing bowl. Cover with plastic wrap and refrigerate at least 4 hours.

6   When ready to serve, stir in vanilla and rum.

7   Pour approximately 8 ounces each into some festive glasses and dust the tops with remaining cinnamon.

* Includes 4 hours cooling time in the refrigerator.

TIPS & OPTIONS

Avoid using flavored rums (spiced, coconut, apple, banana) as manufacturers likely add sugar to the blend. Instead, stick with traditional white or dark rum, which contain 0 grams of net carbs per 1.5 fluid ounce serving.

Serve Wonder If I Won Eggnog warm or cold, your choice.

Increase the amount of protein by adding a scoop of protein powder or puréed tofu to the mixture.

Raw eggs give eggnog a bad rep. Carefully refrigerate unused portions of your eggnog.

Feeling fancy? Insert a cinnamon stick in each cup.

HOT MULLET MARKET CIDER

◗ ✕ ◉ 🍃

<table>
<tr><td>TOTAL COST</td><td>$1.63</td></tr>
<tr><td>COST PER SERVING</td><td>$0.41</td></tr>
</table>

NET CARBS

0G

SERVES 4

PER SERVING:

CALORIES	2
FAT	0G
PROTEIN	0G
SODIUM	0MG
FIBER	0G
CARBOHYDRATES	0G
NET CARBS	0G
SUGAR	0G

TIME

PREP TIME:	5 MINUTES
COOK TIME:	10 MINUTES

TIPS & OPTIONS ⟩⟩

Strain the Hot Mullet Market Cider as soon as it cools. Leaving the whole cloves in will make the cider bitter.

Adjust the sweetener to your taste as well as the amount of apple cider vinegar. If I'm in the mood for a more robust flavor, I add an additional splash of apple cider vinegar to my mug.

Apple cider vinegar is rumored to provide a variety of health benefits: improved complexion, aid with digestion, maintain blood sugar levels, and assist with weight loss. That's quite a reputation!

I couldn't resist with this one. There just aren't enough opportunities to fit the word *mullet* into regular conversation! Unlike the mullet 1980s hairdo, however, Hot Mullet Market Cider will never go out of style. This classic blend of aromatic flavors is here to stay. Have you noticed how much better your sense of smell has gotten since cutting sugar from your diet? Brew up a pot of Hot Mullet Market Cider to celebrate the reawakening of your fifth sense.

3 cups water

6 cinnamon sticks

14 whole cloves

8 (1-gram) packets 0g net carbs sweetener

3 tablespoons apple cider vinegar

1 In a medium pot over medium heat, add water, cinnamon sticks, cloves, and sweetener. Bring to boil and simmer 10 minutes, stirring regularly.

2 Remove from heat and let cool. When liquid is warm but cool enough to drink, add apple cider vinegar and stir to mix.

3 Using strainer to remove seasonings, pour liquid evenly into four glass mugs and serve warm.

LOTTO CHAI LATTE

If black coffee makes you feel too jittery, a cup of Lotto Chai Latte might be a better way to go. It has just one-third the amount of caffeine when compared to a cup of joe, making it a more suitable choice to maintain satiety but *not* cause you to bounce off the walls! Lotto Chai Latte might be new to you, but second to water, chai is one of the oldest drinks in the history of the world.

2 cups water

4 tea bags black tea

3 cinnamon sticks

⅛ teaspoon ground cardamom

⅛ teaspoon allspice

⅛ teaspoon ground anise

1 tablespoon coconut butter

1½ cups unsweetened almond milk

6 (1-gram) packets 0g net carbs sweetener

1 In a small pot over medium heat, boil water. Remove from heat, add tea bags, and steep 5 minutes.

2 Remove tea bags from pot and pour hot tea into a slow cooker. Add remaining ingredients to slow cooker and stir to combine until sweetener is dissolved and all ingredients are well mixed.

3 Put lid on slow cooker and cook on high 2 hours.

4 Remove lid, whisk, and let cool.

5 When cooled, stir again and pour through a strainer into four glass mugs with handles. Serve warm.

TOTAL COST	$2.56
COST PER SERVING	$0.64

NET CARBS

1G

SERVES 4

PER SERVING:	
CALORIES	37
FAT	3G
PROTEIN	1G
SODIUM	72MG
FIBER	1G
CARBOHYDRATES	2G
NET CARBS	1G
SUGAR	0G

TIME

PREP TIME:	10 MINUTES
COOK TIME:	2 HOURS
	5 MINUTES

TIPS & OPTIONS

If you don't have a slow cooker, simmer ingredients in a medium-sized covered pot over low heat for 2 hours, stirring regularly.

Reboot a serving of Homespun Coconut Buttah (see Chapter 8) here as the fat source.

Your preferred fat can be added to make your tea "bulletproof." Popular additives include unsalted butter, ghee, HWC, or half and half.

Increasing fats in your DIRTY, LAZY, KETO diet helps keep you feeling fuller, for longer, but also makes you feel scandalous when you eat them. Eating fat is almost a parlor trick—it helps reduce FOMO and lingering resentment over a reduction in carb intake.

NET CARBS

3G

SERVES 2

PER SERVING:

CALORIES	220
FAT	7G
PROTEIN	4G
SODIUM	433MG
FIBER	1G
CARBOHYDRATES	4G
NET CARBS	3G
SUGAR	2G

TIME

PREP TIME:	5 MINUTES
COOK TIME:	0 MINUTES

TIPS & OPTIONS »

Not a fan of gin? Customize your signature cocktail and make it with your favorite brand of vodka instead.

Much like the benign meaning behind *dirty* in DIRTY, LAZY, KETO, the dirty martini also gets its name from neutral roots. *Dirty* refers to its cloudy appearance brought on by the addition of olive brine to the vermouth and gin cocktail. *Not exactly scandalous!*

If you don't have a professional cocktail shaker on hand (I'm not sure who does), secure plastic wrap over the mouth of a large glass and *shake*.

DIRTY (LAZY, KETO) MINIMUM PAYMENT MARTINI

Every guy or gal needs a signature drink, *don't ya think?* It seems so *glamorous*… Maybe I'm "small-town," but after binge-watching every season of HBO's *Sex and the City*, I'm convinced this is the only way to go. Instead of ordering a pricey Pink Cosmo, however, I'm toasting your weight loss success with a homespun DIRTY (LAZY, KETO) Minimum Payment Martini. Raise your glass for a DIRTY, LAZY, KETO *Cheers!*

2 (1½-ounce) shots unflavored gin

½ ounce olive brine

½ ounce dry vermouth

6 stuffed green olives

2 slices cooked (crispy) no-sugar-added bacon

4 (1") chunks avocado

1 Shake gin, brine, and vermouth together in a large covered glass over a few ice cubes.

2 Strain chilled liquids quickly into two martini glasses (leaving ice behind).

3 Use decorative skewer to pierce (in a fun pattern) olives, bacon, and avocado chunks.

4 Insert skewer into glass as drink stirrer. Serve immediately.

JACKPOT CINNAMON SHOT

TOTAL COST	$0.55
COST PER SERVING	$0.55

NET CARBS

0G

SERVES 1

PER SERVING:

CALORIES	117
FAT	0G
PROTEIN	0G
SODIUM	0MG
FIBER	0G
CARBOHYDRATES	6G
NET CARBS	0G
SUGAR	0G
SUGAR ALCOHOL	5.7G

TIME

PREP TIME:	10 MINUTES
COOK TIME:	0 MINUTES

TIPS & OPTIONS ≫

Sugar-free candy has many creative uses beyond curing a sweet tooth. I keep a secret stash on hand for important moments just like this.

Instead of enjoying this drink as a shot, pour over ice and sip.

Water down the excitement and potency by diluting whiskey with equal parts sugar-free soda water.

I experimented by substituting sugar-free peppermint candy for cinnamon and found the resulting drink quite similar. Then again, I might have had "a few" by then in the name of "cookbook spear-mint-tay-tion."

Nothing says "it's the holidays" like a swill of Fireball, right? The adults in my family sure enjoy a nip of this whiskey (or two!) on special occasions. I enjoyed partaking in that tradition until I learned how much sugar was in one serving. *So not worth it!* It occurred to me I didn't have to miss out on the fun. I could make my own! When a food (or drink) is important to you, find a way to make a substitute or risk feeling resentful. There is always a way!

1½ ounces (1 shot) unflavored Kentucky whiskey

1 piece sugar-free cinnamon candy

1 Pour whiskey into a shot glass.

2 Unwrap candy and drop it into shot glass.

3 Let candy soak for 10 minutes, stirring every couple minutes, then remove it.

4 Enjoy your sugar-free cinnamon-flavored whiskey!

LIQUIDATION BATTERY RECHARGE

Ketosis (and drinking alcohol!) takes its toll on your fluid levels. You need to hydrate, hydrate, hydrate! When pickle juice or sugar-free sports drinks aren't an option, this Liquidation Battery Recharge recipe will save the day. *Your hangover thanks you in advance!*

> 2½ cups water
>
> 3 tablespoons fresh lemon juice
>
> 1 teaspoon apple cider vinegar
>
> 2 (1-gram) packets 0g net carbs sweetener
>
> ½ teaspoon salt
>
> 1 cup ice

1   Combine all ingredients (including the lemon rinds if you squeezed your own juice) in pitcher and stir until sweetener and salt are dissolved.

2   Serve immediately.

TOTAL COST $0.58
COST PER SERVING $0.58

NET CARBS

3G

SERVES 1

PER SERVING:

CALORIES	11
FAT	0G
PROTEIN	0G
SODIUM	1,162MG
FIBER	0G
CARBOHYDRATES	3G
NET CARBS	3G
SUGAR	1G

TIME

PREP TIME:	5 MINUTES
COOK TIME:	0 MINUTES

TIPS & OPTIONS

This large 20+ ounce serving will both hydrate and help replace much needed electrolytes. There is no need to feel sluggish, have foggy thinking, or suffer from a headache (all symptoms of the mythical keto flu) when this simple solution is at your beck and call.

Out of lemon juice? Substitute lime juice instead. The citrus doesn't have to be fresh, either; 100% juice from concentrate will still do the trick!

Feeling under the weather? Omit the ice and enjoy Liquidation Battery Recharge served warm in a mug.

BOXED WINE SANGRIA

Just the thought of trying to "eat clean" 24/7 is enough to make me rebel. Do we really need to eat "perfectly" in order to lose weight? Though controversial, I'd like to respond by yelling, "NO WAY, JOSE!" When consumed responsibly, alcohol and weight loss can coexist. On that note, pour yourself a glass of Boxed Wine Sangria. Note there is even a slice of orange floating on top! #Breaktherules, my friend. *Salud!*

- ½ cup sliced strawberries
- ½ cup blueberries
- ½ cup chopped orange slices
- ¼ (3-liter) box pinot noir wine, or 1 (750-milliliter) bottle pinot noir
- ½ cup unflavored vodka
- ½ cup 0g net carbs sweetener
- 2 cups plain seltzer water, chilled

1   To a small bowl, add strawberries, blueberries, and oranges and partially mash to release flavor.

2   Add all ingredients except seltzer to a large pitcher and stir until sweetener is dissolved and pitcher is well blended. Refrigerate and chill at least 2 hours.

3   Add chilled seltzer and stir again. Serve over ice.

TOTAL COST	$7.41
COST PER SERVING	$0.74

NET CARBS

4G

SERVES 10

PER SERVING:

CALORIES	100
FAT	0G
PROTEIN	0G
SODIUM	4MG
FIBER	0G
CARBOHYDRATES	9G
NET CARBS	4G
SUGAR	2G
SUGAR ALCOHOL	4.8G

TIME

PREP TIME:	10 MINUTES
COOK TIME:	0 MINUTES

TIPS & OPTIONS

There is no need to buy anything expensive here (especially since you'll be mixing the wine with other flavors). Grab some Trader Joe's "Two-Buck Chuck" and *let's get this party started!*

Save money and head to your freezer aisle to buy berries for Boxed Wine Sangria; appearances don't matter here as the berries will be "smashed" upon arrival.

Dry red wines like merlot, pinot noir, and cabernet sauvignon are the lowest in carbs.

Serve Boxed Wine Sangria with Cash Only Chili Relleno (see Chapter 9), *sí*?

ADDITIONAL RESOURCES

- Dirty! For additional free resources, visit https://dirtylazyketo.com/
- Want direct support from Stephanie? Join the private, limited-enrollment Premium DIRTY, LAZY, KETO support group for women only (subscription-based) at www.facebook.com/groups/590158001856505/
- Listen to the author directly on the free podcast *DIRTY, LAZY, Girl*, available wherever you listen to podcasts or at https://dirtylazyketo.com/
- Get involved in the DIRTY, LAZY, KETO community:

  www.facebook.com/dirtylazyketo

  www.facebook.com/groups/DirtyLazyKeto

  www.pinterest.com/dirtylazyketo/

  www.instagram.com/dirtylazyketo/

  www.instagram.com/140lost/

  www.bit.ly/DLKYouTube

  https://twitter.com/140lost

RECIPES RESOURCES

UNDERSTANDING RECIPE ICONS

Throughout the cookbook you'll find special awards that highlight unique attributes of the recipes, such as:

- **Reboot:** It's a *twofer!* Make extra and use part for another meal.
- **I'm Hangry:** Feeling *HANGRY?* High-fiber, large-portioned meals help "slow down" eating.
- **Picky Eaters:** *He likes it! She likes it!* Crowd-pleasing favorites.
- **Fancy Enough for Guests:** *Ooh la la…* Looks impressive and tastes great!
- **Vegetarian-"ish":** *"Kinda" meatless*, but may still call for dairy and/or eggs.
- **Keto Superstars:** *Flick on your lighter!* Legendary rock star recipes take the stage.

CALCULATING RECIPE SERVING SIZES

The exact amount of a serving is clearly spelled out on nutrition labels, but *not* in recipes. Why is that? There are too many variables involved with cooking to provide an exact amount. The size of eggs you use or the size of your pans directly affects how much food is made. But let's not overcomplicate this. In the spirit of Lazy Keto, put away your food scales and measuring cups when estimating what portion to serve yourself. Follow this simple calculation instead:

Divide the recipe quantity by the *yield* to determine the serving size.

If a lasagna serves eight people and has 9 grams of net carbs per serving, cut your lasagna into eight even pieces and enjoy. Each piece of lasagna is a single serving, meaning each piece will contain 9 grams of net carbs. *Easy peasy!*

GLOSSARY

As a courtesy, I've included a glossary of how I am using common keto vocabulary. (Keep in mind that my definitions might be different from what you have heard before.)

KETO AND KETO FACTIONS

DIRTY KETO

Dirty Keto is eating whatever foods you choose within your macro goals or limits (which are different for everyone). Unfortunately, there are a lot of misconceptions about Dirty Keto. Critics are horrified about including junk food or lower-quality meats into one's diet. They assume we survive *solely* on hot dogs and sugar-free Red Bull! *That's just not true.* Instead, Dirty Keto empowers you with more flexible options about what to eat. There is no judgment or strict rules about your lifestyle. You might "eat clean" during the workweek but then live a little on the weekends, for example. Foods aren't demonized either—artificial sweeteners and low-carb substitutes are fair game. Dirty Keto followers don't limit their food or beverage choices and might even be spotted drinking a Diet Coke (*oh, the horror!*).

DIRTY, LAZY, KETO

DIRTY, LAZY, KETO is not just a diet; it's a lifestyle. As a modern hybrid, it reaps the benefits of losing weight, but without limitations of food choices or the obligation of counting every macro. We eat foods that are higher in fat, moderate in protein, and lower in carbs, but allow for a little fun and flexibility. We are open to the idea of artificial sweeteners (Diet Coke or Splenda for example) and include packaged foods (protein bars, low-carb tortillas) in our meals. Dirty *and* Lazy Keto followers count only net carbs. I am the superhero of this category! I even coined the term. *Somebody make me a T-shirt!*

KETO

Keto is simply a shortened word for "ketogenic."

KETO POLICE

Keto police insist Strict Keto rules must be followed at all times! Though they don't wear a uniform, you can easily spot a member of the keto police by their social media posts that frequently ridicule others, arguing, "but THAT'S NOT KETO!" Keto police believe their purity and high standards make them superior; they constantly feel the need to educate and "correct" dissenting keto disciples.

KETOGENIC DIET

The ketogenic diet is a diet of foods high in fat, moderate in protein, and low in carbohydrates, with the goal of putting the body into ketosis.

KETOSIS

Ketosis occurs when the body burns ketones from the liver as the main energy source (as opposed to using glucose as the energy source, derived from carbs). Ketosis is often an indicator (but not a requirement) of weight loss.

LAZY KETO

Lazy Keto followers only count their net carbs intake—not fat grams or protein intake. Lazy Keto does *not* mean unwilling to work hard for weight loss. This term refers to just one style of counting a single macro in keto—the net carb—not a relaxed lifestyle or lack of energy. Not tracking doesn't mean overconsumption, though! Common sense is *always* used.

STRICT KETO

Strict Keto adheres to a rigid and closely monitored ketogenic diet consisting of no more than 20 grams of net carbohydrates per day. Followers insist on organic ingredients and avoid all processed foods. The keto prescription for weight loss never deviates: Calories distributed are distributed to a perfect ratio of 75 percent fat, 20 percent protein, and 5 percent carbohydrates.

If you are not sure what keto camp you fall into, try taking the free, short quiz I created on my website at https://dirtylazyketo.com/quiz/.

RELATED KETO TERMS

CALORIES

Calories are units of heat that food provides to the body. There are no "good" or "bad" calories. You've got to let this one go, people! A calorie is just an innocent unit of measurement, like a cup or a gallon. Our bodies *require* calories to survive. With DIRTY, LAZY, KETO, calories are not the focus (instead, net carbs are). The 1980s are over, my friends, and only counting calories of low-fat foods is just as passé as leg warmers.

CARBOHYDRATES/CARBS

Carbohydrates, or carbs (for short), are sugars, starches, and fibers found in fruits, grains, vegetables, and milk products. Carbohydrates contain 4 calories per gram.

CHAFFLE

Chaffle started off as a portmanteau of "cheese waffles," but the term has since evolved to include a variety of recipes made with a waffle maker. This glorious, addictive bread substitute is made in just a few minutes using a handful of ingredients and cooked inside a waffle iron.

FAT

Fat is the densest form of energy, providing 9 calories per gram. The most obvious example of fat is oil (olive, coconut, sesame, canola, vegetable, and so on). Less clear examples of fats are dairy foods, nuts, avocados, and oily fish. Some fats have a better reputation than others (think about how the media portrays eggs, mayonnaise, Alfredo sauce, or chicken skin). No matter what the quality of the source, *fat is fat is fat*.

FIBER

Fiber is not digested by the body and is removed as waste. There are two types of fiber: soluble and insoluble. Fiber is a complex carbohydrate that does not raise blood sugar. *Fiber is your friend.*

INSOLUBLE FIBER

Insoluble fiber does *not* absorb water. Insoluble fiber moves through the intestine mostly intact, adding bulk to the stool and preventing constipation. Low-carb foods that contain notable amounts of insoluble fiber include blueberries, raspberries, strawberries, raw almonds, flaxseed, sesame seeds, walnuts, Brussels sprouts, cooked kale, and soybeans.

KETO FLU

Keto flu is an avoidable set of symptoms (headache, lethargy, leg cramps) associated with dehydration, often experienced at the onset of the keto diet. Because the metabolic process of ketosis requires more water, increased hydration is required by the body.

MACRONUTRIENTS/MACROS

Macronutrients, or macros, come in three packages: *carbohydrates*, *protein*, and *fat*. All macronutrients are obtained through foods in the diet, as the body cannot produce them. Each macro fulfills vital roles for your health. All macros contain calories but at different densities. Carbohydrates and proteins have 4 calories per gram, and fat has 9 calories per gram.

NET CARBS

Net carbs are the unit of measurement tracked in DIRTY, LAZY, KETO. When looking at a nutrition label, net carbs are calculated by subtracting all fiber and sugar alcohol grams from the listed amount of carbohydrates. Total carbs, minus fiber, minus sugar alcohol, equals net carbs. Net carbs are the leftover carbs in this mathematical equation.

PROTEIN

Protein has 4 calories per gram. Proteins take longer to digest because they are long-chain amino acids. Protein is largely found in meats, dairy foods, eggs, legumes, nuts, and seafood.

SOLUBLE FIBER

Soluble fiber attracts water. When you eat foods high in soluble fiber, it turns to mush inside your body. Soluble fiber, absorbs water quickly and helps to soften stool. It slows down your digestion and helps you to feel full. Examples of low-carb foods with notable amounts of soluble fiber include blackberries, strawberries, flaxseed, psyllium seed husks, artichokes, and soybeans.

SUGAR ALCOHOLS

Sugar alcohols are reduced-calorie sweeteners. They do not contain alcohol. They are commonly used in sugar-free candy and low-carb desserts and are not digested by the body.

US/METRIC CONVERSION CHARTS

VOLUME CONVERSIONS

US VOLUME MEASURE	METRIC EQUIVALENT
⅛ teaspoon	0.5 milliliter
¼ teaspoon	1 milliliter
½ teaspoon	2 milliliters
1 teaspoon	5 milliliters
½ tablespoon	7 milliliters
1 tablespoon (3 teaspoons)	15 milliliters
2 tablespoons (1 fluid ounce)	30 milliliters
¼ cup (4 tablespoons)	60 milliliters
⅓ cup	90 milliliters
½ cup (4 fluid ounces)	125 milliliters
⅔ cup	160 milliliters
¾ cup (6 fluid ounces)	180 milliliters
1 cup (16 tablespoons)	250 milliliters
1 pint (2 cups)	500 milliliters
1 quart (4 cups)	1 liter (about)

WEIGHT CONVERSIONS

US VOLUME MEASURE	METRIC EQUIVALENT
½ ounce	15 grams
1 ounce	30 grams
2 ounces	60 grams
3 ounces	85 grams
¼ pound (4 ounces)	115 grams
½ pound (8 ounces)	225 grams
¾ pound (12 ounces)	340 grams
1 pound (16 ounces)	454 grams

OVEN TEMPERATURE CONVERSIONS

DEGREES FAHRENHEIT	DEGREES CELSIUS
200 degrees F	95 degrees C
250 degrees F	120 degrees C
275 degrees F	135 degrees C
300 degrees F	150 degrees C
325 degrees F	160 degrees C
350 degrees F	180 degrees C
375 degrees F	190 degrees C
400 degrees F	205 degrees C
425 degrees F	220 degrees C
450 degrees F	230 degrees C

BAKING PAN SIZES

AMERICAN	METRIC
8 × 1½ inch round baking pan	20 × 4 cm cake tin
9 × 1½ inch round baking pan	23 × 3.5 cm cake tin
11 × 7 × 1½ inch baking pan	28 × 18 × 4 cm baking tin
13 × 9 × 2 inch baking pan	30 × 20 × 5 cm baking tin
2 quart rectangular baking dish	30 × 20 × 3 cm baking tin
15 × 10 × 2 inch baking pan	30 × 25 × 2 cm baking tin (Swiss roll tin)
9 inch pie plate	22 × 4 or 23 × 4 cm pie plate
7 or 8 inch springform pan	18 or 20 cm springform or loose bottom cake tin
9 × 5 × 3 inch loaf pan	23 × 13 × 7 cm or 2 lb narrow loaf or pate tin
1½ quart casserole	1.5 liter casserole
2 quart casserole	2 liter casserole

INDEX

ABOUT THE AUTHORS

USA TODAY bestselling author and creator of DIRTY, LAZY, KETO, Stephanie Laska doesn't just talk the talk; she *walks the walk*. She is one of the few keto authors who has successfully lost half of her body weight (140 pounds!) and maintained that weight loss for seven years and counting.

Want the "full story" on how you, too, can lose weight for good? Check out the blockbuster *DIRTY, LAZY, KETO®: Get Started Losing Weight While Breaking the Rules*, the guidebook that started an international trend to help hundreds of thousands of fans lose weight in a new way.

Expect humor, honesty, and inspiration from your DLK girlfriend, Stephanie Laska. Her mission is to help as many people as possible fight obesity *one carb at a time!* She fights back against the shame, blame, and judgment surrounding obesity with DIRTY, LAZY, KETO.

Stephanie's honest sass and fresh approach to the keto diet break all the traditional rules of dieting. You might have caught her televised cooking debut with Al Roker on NBC's *Today* show. Her story and image have been celebrated in articles or images shared by Fox News, *US News & World Report, New York Post, Reader's Digest, Yahoo! News, First for Women, Woman's World, Muscle & Fitness: Hers, Keto for You*, runDisney, and *Costco Connection*. She has run a dozen marathons, most notably the New York City Marathon as a sponsored athlete from PowerBar. Not bad for a girl who ran her first mile (as in ever!) close to age forty.

Alongside her coauthor and husband, William Laska, Stephanie has created more support tools: *The DIRTY, LAZY, KETO® Cookbook: Bend the Rules to Lose the Weight!* and *DIRTY, LAZY, KETO® Fast Food Guide: 10 Carbs or Less.* Coming soon! *The DIRTY, LAZY, KETO® No Time to Cook Cookbook* (Simon & Schuster, 2021). Stephanie also hosts a free weekly podcast, *DIRTY, LAZY, Girl,* available for listening wherever you currently listen to podcasts.

Stephanie and Bill reside in sunny California. When they aren't talking about their third child (DIRTY, LAZY, KETO), the Laskas enjoy running, traveling "on the cheap," and shopping at thrift stores.